Show Your Money Who's Boss

Taming The Money Monster

J. Barry Wood

Copyright © 2010 J. Barry Wood
All rights reserved.

ISBN: 1-4392-3919-3
ISBN-13: 9781439239193

To order additional copies, please contact us.
BookSurge
www.booksurge.com
1-866-308-6235

Table of Contents

Introduction	ix
Part 1: It's Like Giving Yourself a Raise	1
1. Finding Hidden Money	3
2. Picking up Diamonds	9
Part 2: Taming the Money Monsters of…	19
3. Unemployment	21
4. Joblessness	29
5. Business Failure	37
6. Layoffs	45
7. Terminations	55
8. Budget Busters	61
9. Financial Crises	75
10. Panic	99
11. Debt	111
12. Payday	119
13. "Lone Ranger"	133
14. Decision-Making	141

PART 3: TURBO CHARGE YOUR MONEY	**155**
15. GOD'S PROMISES AND ANSWERED PRAYERS	**157**
16. SHOW YOUR MONEY WHO'S BOSS	**173**
17. RECEIVING GOD'S WILDEST XTREME BLESSINGS	**187**
18. TAKE CHARGE OF YOUR FUTURE	**197**
19. BECOMING THE SUCCESSFUL PERSON YOU WERE MEANT TO BE	**207**

Introduction: *Show Your Money Who's Boss* was written to empower you to be the master of your money. It will enable you to…

- regain control over your finances
- bring joy back into your financial life
- direct your money to serve you
- replace financial uncertainty with peace
- be rescued from your daily money struggles
- enjoy spending without guilt
- be refreshed in your heart, mind, and soul with strength

Show Your Money Who's Boss will show you how to tame the Money Monsters of…

- not having enough money
- joblessness
- layoffs
- financial crises
- panic
- being overwhelmed by debt
- financial ADHD
- credit problems
- deficit spending
- skimpy retirement

Show Your Money Who's Boss is not just another boring money book designed to put readers to sleep. To the contrary, it is an exciting lifestyle! A journey toward financial peace and prosperity, it can enable you to eliminate the following types of statements from your financial life: "I just don't know where my money goes. I am sick and tired of living paycheck to paycheck. I dread balancing my checkbook. And, I feel like my money is controlling me."

Your money is supposed to be serving you and your needs. It is not there to be served by you. How refreshing it would be to replace the uncertainties of this turbulent financial world with confidence, and enjoy freedom from the day-to-day struggles money problems bring with them. Have some fun and learn as I did that one of the best decisions I ever made was the decision to Show My Money Who's Boss.

JBW

Part 1
It's Like Giving Yourself a Raise

Chapter 1
Finding Hidden Money

Mary just inherited a fully-furnished old Victorian two-story house from her elderly Aunt Bessie who had never married. While moving in, Mary was placing some things in the attic and noticed something that looked like an old letter taped to one of the rafters. She opened the envelope and began to read. Her heart pounded wildly. Mary knew that Aunt Bessie was a bit eccentric and had a weird sense of humor. Her screams of surprise and joy brought her husband, Bud, to her rescue. He read the letter aloud. Though it was short, it triggered an emotional response in both of them that they hadn't had in years.

Mary, since you are reading this letter I know that you now have possession of my dear old house. Since you are my only descendent I have left it to you and your family to enjoy for as long as you live. In order for you to enjoy your time here and to remember me, I have left a lot of money for you to use. You know that I never trusted banks all that much…so I hid all my money, $100,000, in many places throughout the house and yard. As you hunt for it, remember me. To get you started…look under that loose board in the floor over by the chimney.
Love, Aunt Bessie

Mary took Bud over to the chimney, lifted the loose board and pulled out a metal box. Their hearts pounded harder than ever, and their hands were trembling. When they opened the lid they were dumbfounded. Bud pulled out a wad of $100 dollar bills. He counted it, and it totaled $10,000. They looked at one another and embraced in sheer joy…they knew that there was another $90,000 awaiting them. The treasure hunt was on!

Bud and Mary were so thrilled. They would lie awake in bed at night planning their European and Hawaiian vacations. They decided on what kind of new car to buy. They talked about buying some new furniture, and one day after work they rushed out and bought a new big-screen TV. Then they started their search. They searched all the easy places first. They searched the entire house from top to bottom. They found money! Wow, did they ever find money. They found two quarters, three dimes, a nickel, and eleven pennies. They found a whopping ninety-six cents. At first they were a little mad, but they crashed on the couch and began laughing. They even made fun of each other by mimicking one another crawling around on the floor looking for loose boards, tapping the walls listening for hollow spots, and checking the stairs for any loose steps. They laughed and laughed so loudly they were afraid that the neighbors would come over to check on them. They even thought of putting their antics on the Internet to let the whole world share in their fun. But they dare not tell anyone about the money. The money was theirs, and they were going to find it no matter what it took.

The next night Bud and Mary sat down after dinner to develop a plan. This time they were serious about finding the money. Mary reminded Bud about the Hawaiian vacation they wanted to take and the red convertible he would soon be driving. The next day was Saturday so they spent all day in the back yard digging. Even Skippy, their beautiful Cocker Spaniel got in on the act. They dug and dug and dug. They dug up every shrub and every tree in the entire back yard. The yard looked like a construction site or a road construction project...potholes everywhere. No money. This time they collapsed on the couch and rubbed one another's sore backs and aching arms and legs.

Somehow they were energized. Again, they broke out in laughter. This time they were thinking how silly they must have looked to the neighbors...digging up half the back yard; chasing one another and Skippy around the yard, throwing dirt in the air and on each other. They took hot baths and fell into bed and into a sound sleep. They got up early the next morning and planned their day. They would go to McDonalds for brunch, go to church, and then come back home to hunt treasure. Away they went.

Bud and Mary had a great time that day looking for the cash. They started in the back upstairs bedroom and began systematically ripping up every single board in the floor. Nothing. Next, they ripped away the door facings, the baseboards and the crown moldings. Nothing. They had spent the entire day searching for money, but came up empty handed. Off to bed, to work the next morning, and back to rip the plaster walls apart that night. Nothing. Tuesday night they moved to the second upstairs bedroom and went through the entire procedure all over again. Nothing. By Wednesday morning they were frustrated. One back yard and two rooms down and six rooms and a front yard to go. Bud thought it sounded a little like a fourth-quarter drive by the Green Bay Packers. Mary and Bud were beginning to get a little obsessed by the time they finished the second bedroom. By the time they tackled the dining room their nerves were frayed. Still, zip, nada, nothing.

Was this some kind of cruel joke Aunt Bessie was playing on them? In her frustration, Mary ripped one of the drapes off the wall, and voila, several $20s flew out of its hem. She ripped into the hem and pulled out a couple of $50s and a lone $100 dollar bill. They stayed up all night going through every room and every drape in the house. When the sun came up they had a stack of cash that totaled $6,700. They were so excited that Bud put a lampshade on his head and danced around the living room like a wealthy sheik. Mary joined in as they danced all over the room knocking over lamps and a couple of chairs. She grabbed her phone and captured some video of Bud going crazy, and then joined him in dancing again.

They had a great day together. They threw the money into the air and felt like they were on top of the world; dear Aunt Bessie must be smiling down on them from Heaven. The next day they decided to go through every closet in the house. They hit the jackpot again. Money was hidden in the pockets of Aunt Bessie's old coats and clothes. They meticulously searched every single article of clothing in the house. They found shoe boxes and old shoes with money inside them. They felt like they were getting rich. By the end of the day they had found another $7,362 in cash.

The next day they combed over every square inch of that house again and again. No more money. They both took the week off from work and spent the entire time looking inside every picture frame, inside every lamp, inside every piece of furniture, but they found no money except for a few coins that had fallen into the couch and chairs…exactly $3.27 in change. They were frustrated. Last week had yielded $14,062 from the drapes, old clothes, and three shoe boxes. This week had yielded $3.27.

On Saturday night they decided to go back to plan A: start ripping up the floors and ripping apart the walls of the remaining five rooms. Monday night after work they started in the back upstairs bedroom. Two days were spent in that room, but they had no new money. They spent all the next week ripping their way through two more rooms. Nothing. By now a month had passed and Bud and Mary were doing little else except dismantling the house from the inside out. They read and re-read Aunt Bessie's letter. Somewhere in that house or yard was another $75,938.

They decided that they had to be getting close…they were down to their last two rooms and the front yard. Since they hadn't found any money in the floors, walls, and ceilings, they decided to tackle the front yard the next Saturday. But, this time they had a plan. They would hire some of the kids from the youth group at church and have them come over early Saturday morning to plant some new shrubs and trees. Four guys rolled up in a pickup truck on Saturday morning. Bud told them to start by digging up all the shrubs in the front flower beds. By 10:00 AM there were no more living shrubs in their yard. Nothing. Bud and the guys planted new shrubs till noon, and Mary served sandwiches and lemonade for lunch. After lunch they spent the rest of the day digging up trees and planting new ones in the front yard and re-digging the beds in the back yard, just in case they had missed something. As the day ended, Bud had shelled out $595 for assorted shrubs, trees, and bushes and another $400 to the four guys for a total of $995. Not bad for a Saturday of yard work. Though the yard looked much better, Mary remarked that they had "nothing" to show for it.

They counted once again: $24,062 down and $75,938 to go. It had to be somewhere inside their house. As the day drew to a close

Mary told Bud that she was going to take a hot bath and asked him to sit down and map out their next move. She got in the bubble-filled tub and he crashed on the couch...and then it hit them both at the same time...the bathtub. The very last place in the house Aunt Bessie would think that a burglar would look. That had better be it because that was about all that was left besides the kitchen. Mary jumped out, Bud jumped up off the couch, and together they grabbed pry bars and ripped the tub up from the floor.

Finally, there it was. Another metal box exactly like the one they had found in the attic one month earlier. This time they knew that they had hit the "Mother Load." Both shrieked and screamed with uncontrollable joy. They knew that all their work had been worth it. Sure, they had destroyed the house, making it almost unlivable, but now it was time for the vacation and the sports car...but the box was locked. There was no key. Bud tried and tried but couldn't pry it open. In desperation, Mary slammed the box onto the floor again and again. Finally it popped open and money spilled out all over the floor...real money, real green money. They counted it. It didn't take long because there was a total of fifty-eight one dollar bills. They both began to scream and shriek again. This time, their screams were screams of unimaginable frustration. They were both on the verge of being totally uncontrollable; Bud began screaming like a lunatic and started hitting the bathtub with the pry bar. Mary was pounding the floor with her fists and was pulling her hair. Skippy was running around in circles chasing his tail, snapping at Bud, and howling fiercely.

Suddenly, Mary spied another letter neatly folded and beside the box. She ripped it open and began reading aloud:

Mary, I'm happy that you found this last treasure box. I hope you are not too disappointed. When I finished saving my money I put $75,000 inside this little box. Then I gradually began to spend it. Do you remember that vacation I took to Italy a few years ago? Then I went to Hawaii, and when I came home, I bought my friend Earl a nice little red convertible. He and I really had a wonderful time riding around with the top down. By the time I hid this box under the tub it was almost empty. Sorry, but I hope that the $10,000 from the attic will

help you. After all, you were my favorite niece, and at least you have the house to enjoy.
Love, Aunt Bessie

    The story you just read was based upon a true story from my wife's family. There really was an Aunt Bessie, and she really did hide a lot of money in her old house. My wife and I actually spent a week in that house in Houston, Texas while Bessie was still alive. Much of Bessie's money was found and, no doubt, some of it remained in the house when the family sold it. The family actually did get to go on a treasure hunt and they did have a lot of fun searching for and finding several thousand dollars in cash.
    What is the possibility you could find hidden money lying around your house?

Chapter 2
Picking Up Diamonds

HUNT FOR TREASURE

When my children were young I would initiate a game we called "treasure hunt." The game went something like this. One of them would have done an exceptional job at something and I would reward their accomplishment with a small gift or a small amount of money. I would begin by hiding the gift and telling them that they had a reward awaiting them. All they had to do was to find it. I would give them the first clue and send them on a treasure hunt. In advance, I had written and hidden six to eight clues scattered in various places throughout the house. The first clue might be a note hidden under their pillow. It would read: "Look in your sock drawer." They would go to their sock drawer, pull it open and find the second clue: "Look in the bathtub." They would race to the bathtub and find the third clue: "Look under something soft in the den." Once they had found that clue they would read: "Look high and look low in your room to find the next clue." They would search their room and finally locate the clue: "Go outside and look under the doormat." That clue might read: "Look in the back seat of the car," and there they would find a new pair of sneakers, a toy, or some money. They absolutely loved their treasure hunts and still talk about them to this day.

WANT TO HUNT FOR TREASURE OF YOUR OWN?

If you want to show your money who's boss and begin taming the money monsters, consider accepting the challenge to embark upon one of the world's most important treasure hunts. No, you won't be looking for the Hope Diamond or a metal box full of $100 dollar bills, but you will be looking for real cash, and the cash is right there under your very nose. This treasure hunt will take place right in your own home, and you may actually find several thousand dollars in hidden cash. You will determine just how much money you will find. You can find a little or you can find a lot; it will be entirely up to you. Throughout history, some fortunate people have discovered diamond beds lying on top of the ground. Deposited there by ancient volcanic lava flows, diamonds have been found lying on top of the ground waiting for someone to pick them up. Chances are pretty good that you will be able to find cash of your own in some very obvious places right in your own home or business.

Take the time to look around your home and business. Put on your God-given thinking cap. Opportunities abound that can lead you to find money you didn't even know you had. Your newly found money can help ease your budget crunch. Take advantage of the head start and financial successes this book will suggest by identifying some of the money that is right in front of you. Perhaps it will trigger other ideas you can use to improve your finances.

As you read the following possibility list, choose the opportunities that best match your financial situation. If you have a family, involve them in your journey. Seek their input, listen to their feedback, and enlist their help when you are ready to implement new strategies. When your spouse and kids buy into these strategies *before* you start using them, your chances of success will be much greater than if you announce that you have a new set of rules to be followed. Consider meeting with extended family members and friends to bounce your ideas off them. They will likely have some great ideas of their own that are not on the list.

Most importantly, seek God's will and direction as you study the following list. Put a check mark beside the possibilities that might work for you and that would be beneficial to you and your family. Have some fun dreaming about your future. God wants to bless you. Ask him to lead you as you prayerfully study these money-finding opportunities.

Get Excited about Picking Up Your Share of Diamonds

There are hundreds of ways to find your share of diamonds. You may not be able to go on a treasure hunt like Mary and Bud, but you have the potential to discover hundreds, if not thousands of dollars. Without a doubt, the best place to start is to start by deciding that you will get excited! Get excited, and make this an enjoyable activity for yourself and your family. It may seem awkward or even silly at first, but once you get into it, you will become invigorated by all the money you are able to find. If you want to show your money who's boss, you can find thousands of dollars hidden within the ideas included in the pages that follow. Add to these lists the ideas you and your family come up with and before you know it, you will be amazed at the amount of money you may find.

Consider some of the starter ideas that follow:

AUTOMOBILE
- park one car, truck, or SUV
- sell a vehicle
- carpool everywhere you possibly can: work, school, shopping, family outings
- sell your expensive car and buy a cheaper one
- delay trading for another vehicle for as long as possible
- buy a 1-2 year old car
- avoid buying another new car, let someone else take the $5,000 depreciation
- get a tune-up on your vehicle
- conserve as much gasoline as possible
- buy only half a tank at a time, don't carry all the excess weight around
- consolidate your errands to one or two days per week
- buy a less expensive grade of gasoline if your owner's manual approves
- park your car and take a bus or train to work
- walk to work, to school, to church, or to the grocery
- ride your bicycle to work
- walk on errands if possible
- observe the speed limit
- air car's tires to manufacturer's recommended levels
- never lease a vehicle

ENTERTAINMENT
- make saving money a game with your kids and curtail spending
- go to the movies…drag out your old home movies

- rediscover reading
- play charades
- eliminate premium channels
- cancel pay-per-view channels
- rent $1.00 movies from the Internet
- invite neighbors over for a night of board games or to watch a movie together
- stop smoking $2-10K per person per year
- stop drinking $2-10K per person per year
- reminisce by retelling the old family stories and creating some new ones
- hand-make your Birthday, Anniversary, Christmas, and holiday cards
- use local library for books, magazines, and videos

Family

- solicit your kids' ideas, and be up front with them about your personal financial crisis
- baby-sit for other couples and reciprocate the favor, or charge money
- institute family nights…stay at home, cook, eat, play games, read, listen to music
- get back to the real meaning of Christmas, don't splurge with gift-giving
- save on gift-giving, instead of giving 40 family gifts, give one. here's how: place 40 names in a hat, draw one, and give that person a gift, you'll get one too
- use that old artificial Christmas tree and unplug the lights except when at home
- skip all the outside lights next Christmas
- stay at home for a holiday, give food to a less fortunate family
- have smaller but more meaningful birthday parties
- invest in some good board games for family nights
- learn to love, appreciate and be friends with your family all over again

- cancel gym or health club membership if not actively using
- cancel country club membership

Food

- eat out a LOT less…once a week
- bake pizza and cookies at home with the family
- cook most meals at home, add up what you spend eating out each week x 52
- pack your lunch for work or school
- cook brownies or cookies to sell to friends, at church, at the office, or at school
- cook more staples-beans, rice, and potatoes
- buy store-brand foods
- buy food in bulk quantities when possible
- keep feeding your pet but buy a less expensive pet food
- use the microwave more than the oven
- eat leftovers instead of chunking them
- eat less meat, veggies are cheaper
- buy less fast food and brown-bag healthy meals
- plan meals for the entire week
- create a shopping list and strictly stick to it

General

- stop ALL unnecessary spending
- delay ALL major purchases
- take a stay-at-home vacation, go to a relative's house, or vacation near your home
- stay at home more
- instead of going shopping, read a good book
- cut back on magazine subscriptions….share a newspaper with a neighbor
- get involved in your church, your kid's school, or a service organization
- volunteer in a nursing home, hospital, or assisted living facility….you can help others
- teach your kids more responsibility

- teach them how, then get them to help with laundry, chores, and yard work
- take a daily vitamin, exercise, and get in shape to save on future health costs
- keep that old computer another year or two
- don't use your printer unnecessarily
- refill your own ink cartridges
- look for ways to tighten your financial belt
- if in school, seek a scholarship
- think, come up with your own ideas to save money and to make money
- save energy at work…walk up flights of stairs

Household

- find a less expensive house or apartment
- save electricity, turn off the TV and rediscover your family
- wash more clothes per load
- dry clothes outside or hang to dry inside
- adjust the settings on your thermostat
- recycle everything you possibly can
- caulk around windows, doors, vent pipes, and spigots
- cover the outside of windows with clear plastic to create a storm window
- winterize your home by applying weather stripping around windows and doors
- wear warmer clothes inside
- take shorter, cooler showers
- turn off all unnecessary lights
- change to energy efficient light bulbs
- learn to sew and do clothing repairs
- make your kid's clothes
- have a garage sale
- cut consumption: start with utilities, cell phone, text messaging, cable and satellite TV
- cut out all pay per view spending
- limit use of your fireplace….it really draws tons of household heat up the chimney

- close off unused rooms of your house, including the heat and AC registers
- use an extra blanket on the bed
- use an electric blanket or bed warmer and turn down the thermostat

Money and Finances
- pay your bills on time
- contact your creditors if you are late with a payment
- contact your credit card company and ask for a lower interest rate
- DON'T borrow money
- DON'T lend money
- budget your income and live it
- don't sell your stocks and bonds; you haven't lost the money until you sell them
- save as much money as you possibly can
- cut ALL frivolous spending
- continue giving to your church, what if everyone quits giving?

Out of the Box
- organize a neighborhood meeting with the agenda of brainstorming money-saving ideas
- organize a barter system in your neighborhood, building, work, school, or church…trade your goods and services for theirs
- clean your landlord's house, or apartments in exchange for rent or rent reduction
- other ideas of your own

Sell Excess Stuff
- sell an extra TV
- sell unneeded items on an Internet auction
- sell a friend's items on an Internet auction for a percentage of the sale
- sell recyclable metals, plastics, newsprint, etc.

- sell your second car or truck
- sell a working and usable appliance
- sell usable furniture
- sell one of your collections
- sell unwanted clothes and household items, and team up with neighbors to have a mega garage sale

Shopping
- shop at thrift stores
- cut trips to your favorite coffee store to one per week
- use grocery and other coupons
- reduce your cell phone plan to the bare-bones plan
- buy generic prescriptions
- shop once a week, less trips to store saves money

Travel
- save $2,000 by planning a stay at home vacation
- plan a short vacation to visit family or friends
- shop online for cheaper airfares, hotels, and rental cars

Volunteer
- save someone else some money by volunteering at a church, school, hospital, assisted living facility, or nursing home
- spend your vacation performing local community service

Add Your Own Ideas Here…

Buy into the Concept of Hidden Treasure

In his parable about the Pearl of Great Price, Matthew 13:45-47, Jesus talked about a man on a search for hidden treasure. "Again, the kingdom of heaven is like a merchant looking for fine pearls. When he found one of great value, he went away and sold everything he had and bought it." In Jesus' parable the hidden treasure was Heaven and the man found it by searching diligently until he found it.

I am asking you to buy only one thing…buy into the concept of finding your own hidden treasure and using it for your family's benefit. The average family can put many of these ideas to work immediately.

Some may require a lot more attention, planning, and forethought. Think these ideas over. Talk about them with your family. Pencil in how much money you think you could save by implementing the ideas you checked. This will give you an idea how much hidden money you can expect to find right in front of you. A word of caution: proceed cautiously. You can jump right in a dramatic fashion and put your family into shock. Or, you can choose to solicit their input and spare your family a lot of unnecessary grief. Either way, please know that change can be painful. It can be especially painful when your family decides to do without something it has always enjoyed. You be the judge as to how to best implement these ideas in your individual situation.

Now that you have studied these lists it is time to have some fun dreaming about your future. God really does want to bless you. "For I know the plans I have for you, plans to prosper you and not to harm you, plans to give you hope and a future" Jeremiah 29:11.

The Lord wants you to prosper financially. A major step toward financial prosperity is learning how to manage the monies God has entrusted into your care. Use this list as a starting point and add ideas of your own. Ask God to lead you as you embark on your journey to find your hidden money. It can be a fun and prosperous journey. Happy hunting!

Show Your Money Who's Boss cannot solve any of your problems, but it may serve as a valuable resource to stimulate some money-finding ideas that you may use as a springboard to help you weather your personal financial storms.

Part 2
Taming the Money Monsters

Chapter 3
Taming the Unemployment Monster

"It was the best of times, it was the worst of times," wrote Charles Dickens in his 1859 classic, *A Tale of Two Cities*. Today, very few would say that these are the best of times. The only ones saying that would be a few hundred Wall Streeters, oil and gold speculators, retiring company executive CEOs with their golden parachutes, and some of the recipients of the TARP and ARRA bailout monies of 2008-2009.

With 14.25 million, or 10% of Americans unemployed on January 1, 2010, almost everyone would say that these are among the worst of times experienced by most people living in the United States. (To make matters worse, experts say that if the Bureau of Labor Statistics' unemployment statistics included both those who have given up searching for jobs, and those who have given up their search for full-time employment to take temporary part-time jobs, the true January 2010 unemployment rate would stand at 17.3 %.)

Due to great economic uncertainty and instability experts agree that for many, the prospects for employment are bleak for most of 2010. Since World War II, the unemployment rate has not passed the dreaded double-digit mark of 10%. It climbed to 10.1% in October 2009, and has continued to hover at or above 10% since that time. Although governmental deficit spending has continued to increase exponentially, inflation is on the horizon, and tremendous tax increases are proposed (should President Obama's Health Care Plan see enactment in 2010,) there is still hope!

This book was written to offer hope. A hope embodied in an approach that can enable readers to once again regain a sense of control over their finances and thus, their very lives themselves.

During the Great Depression of 1929-1941, a full 25% of the American workforce was unemployed. No jobs were available. There are many pockets within America where jobs are not available. One such place is Moraine, Ohio, a town of 8,000 near Columbus, Ohio. Along with the usual jobs found in any town across America, Moraine's largest employer was the General Motors Moraine Assembly Truck Plant. At the end of 2008 the plant closed, leaving 5,000 unemployed people looking for jobs in Moraine and the greater Columbus area. In the wake of GM's Moraine plant closing was the closing of several automotive parts suppliers in the Dayton area who supplied the assembly plant. Those plants employed an additional 3,500 people who are now without jobs.

Common sense dictates that there are not enough jobs to re-employ those 8,500 plus people. Many of those wonderful Americans face unemployment for an extended period of time with no realistic possibility of finding a job in the immediate future. Moraine is joined by dozens of other automotive cities and towns that have experienced closings of automotive assembly or supplier plants as well.

In December 2008, President George Bush announced a unilateral $17.4 billion rescue package for troubled U.S. Auto makers allowing them to forestall bankruptcy. Mr. Bush stated: "In the midst of a financial crisis…allowing the U.S. auto industry to collapse is not a responsible course of action." General Motors responded: "We appreciate the president extending a financial bridge at this most critical time for the U.S. Automotive industry and our nation's economy. This action helps to preserve many jobs, and supports the continued operation of GM and the many suppliers, dealers and small businesses across the country that depends on us." In 2009, President Barack Obama had the option of either administering the rescue package as it existed or of developing one of his own. He did both.

Earlier in December 2008, Chrysler announced plans to shut down all its plants for a period of one month, leaving some 46,000 people temporarily unemployed. In an effort to stave-off bankruptcy, GM announced plans to close its plants for the summer of 2009. Ford followed suit by announcing that it was closing at least 10 plants. In response to the White House's announced rescue package, the Ford

Motor Company indicated that it would not need any of the rescue funds being made available by the Federal Government. Chrysler and General Motors accepted approximately 85 billion dollars in rescue funds. By early June, Ford was the only surviving member of the big-three US auto makers who had not filed for bankruptcy. Chrysler filed for bankruptcy on April 30, 2009, General Motors filed on June 1, 2009, and the government took control of both companies.

In the time since Chrysler and General Motors declared bankruptcy, tens of thousands of people have lost their jobs, and some 3,000 automotive dealerships have either closed or had their relationships severed from Chrysler or GM. Since both corporations filed Chapter 11 bankruptcies, each hopes to restructure and come back with a streamlined and financially successful business model. Now that the US government has taken over two-thirds of the American auto industry, everyone is waiting to see what will be the eventual outcome. Turbulent waters lie ahead. While no one knows the final results of these major decisions by these two automotive giants, all of America is pulling for their survival.

The prospects of tens of thousands of people out of work all at once reminds one of the popular TV program, American Idol, that auditions thousands of Americans for the chance to stand before Simon, Paula, Randy and Kara. In the end, perhaps 50 make it to the televised portion of the auditions, while about half of those make it into the final running. A ratio of 40,000 to 50 does not offer a great chance that someone will be on TV and win the hearts of millions of Americans when they are declared the winner.

If you are applying for a job where 1,000 other people have applied, your chances of being hired are slim. The cruel reality is that many will be unable to find jobs. So many have tried and tried and tried some more but can't find jobs. Add to the mix the 1.25 million people who have either been late with their mortgage payments or are in foreclosure. Almost everyone knows someone who is struggling desperately to get out of financial quicksand.

One of the major steps to showing your money who's boss is that of taming the money monster of joblessness, or gaining control of your job situation. This includes several possibilities, including: retaining the job you already have, searching for a new job, starting your own business, and others.

Setting the Stage to Begin to Show Your Money Who's Boss

If you are employed...

1. Be Thankful for Your Job

Some statistics indicate that more than two thirds of American workers are dissatisfied with their jobs. But, there are millions of people who are desperate to have a job exactly like yours. You may not have a perfect job, very few people do. You may dislike your job, you have a terrible boss, your pay may be crummy, and you may feel that you are under-employed, but you still have a job. With millions of unemployed people looking for work, be thankful for your job.

2. Work Hard to Keep Your Job

You may have to fight to keep your job. No, not a physical or verbal fight, but a fight as outlined in Chapter six: *Taming the Layoff Monster*. Do everything within your power to remain employed. There are some exceptions, but times of economic distress are not usually good times to change jobs.

3. Take a Second Job or Start Your Own Business

If you find that you are running out of paycheck before running out of bills, you may wish to consider finding a part-time second job. The extra money could ease your financial pains and enable you to gain control of your financial situation. If you choose to explore starting your own business there are many ideas for your consideration just ahead.

If You are Unemployed...

4. Don't Blame Yourself

There is no future in blaming yourself for losing your job. It was not your fault that the economy suffered a seismic downturn. Nor is it your fault that your company laid off half its workforce or shut down altogether. Don't waste your energy blaming yourself or wondering what happened. It happened. There is hope. Things will get better someday. Until things improve and you find a job, start by collecting your unemployment benefits. No, it won't be a lot of money but it certainly will help.

5. Don't Fall into Satanic Traps

Divorce: Unfortunately, divorce will become more rampant than ever during the upcoming years. People will blame their spouses for what has happened. Nerves will fray, tempers will flare, and shouting will ensue. You initially married your spouse because you loved them. Rather than turn on them now, go back to the beginning days of your relationship and renew your vows and commitments. Partner or team-up with them to work yourselves out of your crisis. Resist the urge to push them away or blame them for what has happened. Offer understanding, acceptance, and unconditional love.

Abuse: When anger and frustration set in, it is natural that the temptations for verbal, physical, or emotional abuse could emerge. Know this in advance. Talk to the Lord and your family about it. Head it off before it has a chance to begin. You have no right to abuse anyone for any reason. Nor does anyone have the right to abuse you. Don't abuse anyone, and don't allow anyone to abuse you.

Emotional Cruelty: When relationships undergo great stress, emotional cruelty directed toward one's spouse and children is a possibility. Unemployment and the financial hardships it brings rank right up there with the death of a loved one. Things can quickly sour in relationships undergoing extreme duress. Emotional cruelty is most often expressed in tones of voice, hard looks, frowns, sarcasm, silent treatment, hatefulness, and many other ways. Guard against these traps.

Suicide: Desperation, despondency, and terrible economic stresses may contribute to a rise in incidents of suicide. This is the ultimate satanic trick because it robs a person of one of their most precious gifts…life itself. If you are contemplating suicide, PLEASE DON'T DO IT. Seek help from a professional counselor, a clergyman, or a trusted friend.

GIVING UP: Thoreau said: "Most men lead lives of quiet desperation and go to the grave with the song still in them." You may have suffered great loss. Your losses may be accompanied by the loss of the will to go on. If you have given up, this book is filled with hope. There are many reasons to keep going. Allow the Lord to renew your spirit.

6. BE REALISTIC IN YOUR ASSESSMENT

Be totally realistic and honest about your employment possibilities. You may face an extended period of unemployment. No one can say how long it will be before the economy turns around. One of the best things you can do for yourself is to be truthful and honest about your situation. That can lead to acceptance, and acceptance can lead you toward being better able to cope with your unemployment.

7. THIS IS GUT-CHECK TIME

This may be the toughest one of all. It will hurt for you to read these words, but you have to be real. Sugar-coating what has happened to you is not the answer. There WILL be: PAIN, HURT, DISAPPOINTMENT, FRUSTRATION, ANGER, BLAME, and many other issues you will have to deal with. They are unavoidable. No one is coming to bail you out. Unlike the federal government, you don't have the option of printing more money for yourself and your family. You will have to tough it out. It won't be easy. The Marines have a saying: "When the going gets tough, the tough get going." Now is the time for us all to get tough.

8. CALL UPON YOUR NETWORK

You have a network. Use it. Call upon your family, friends, church, civic and social club members, alumni association, local job banks, and Internet job sites. Call upon everyone you know. Exhaust every single possibility. Many of them may be in the same situation as you but at least you can give one another moral support. Ask your closest friends to become advocates for you…to talk to their bosses about you. There are still jobs out there. You may be one of the fortunate who will find one of them. If you possess a unique skill or trade, have highly desirable experience, abilities, or education, talk to a recruiter who can potentially help you with job placement. The key is to get your name before the right people. Networking has worked for millions of people for thousands of years. It may work for you.

9. Write a Resume and Pound the Pavement

Construct a concise, accurate, well-designed, job-specific, attractive, resume and mail or hand-deliver it to dozens of friends and potential places of employment. A successful strategy used by many people is that of designing more than one type of resume. You use virtually the same information; you just package it several different ways to suit various applications. Write a letter telling the company that you will be sending your resume, send it, and follow it up with a phone call or a personal visit to make sure they received it. Tell them that you are available and ask them to schedule an interview with you.

How do you handle Living in an economy where jobs are very tough to find? Lets examine that scenario.

Chapter 4
Taming the Joblessness Monster

"There are simply no jobs out there," remarked Tony to his wife after a day of pounding the pavement. Michelle responded: "I guess you will need to create one of your own." As soon as the words came out of her mouth, she realized that she had turned on the light for both of them. They spent the evening talking over the possibilities of starting a business of their own. They had never thought of themselves as potential business owners, but the more they talked the more apparent it became that starting their own business might just be their best option. Put yourself in their place and explore the possibility of starting your own business.

As you read the following jobs possibility list, look for opportunities that best match your skills, talents, and gifts. Be realistic and do only the things you are equipped to do; for example, don't attempt to practice law unless you are an attorney. If you have a family, be sure to involve them as you search for a job or contemplate starting your own business. Seek their wisdom, listen to their feedback, and enlist their help. God may speak to you through one of them, or he may speak to them through you.

Do yourself a favor by meeting with extended family members and friends who can act as a sounding board for your ideas. If you are brave, and can take it, ask them to be totally honest and tell you what they really think about the job possibilities you are considering. They may even offer suggestions that would help you in finding employment or starting a business. Most importantly, seek God's will and direction before you delve into some new business venture or begin offering a service to others. Prayerfully study these possibilities and have some fun dreaming about your future. God wants to bless you. Ask the Lord to lead you as you explore his will for your life.

HIDDEN JOB OPPORTUNITIES

There are hundreds of ways to find hidden job opportunities. You have the potential to turn your skills and expertise into jobs that will pay you for your abilities or knowledge. Explore things you would like to do and are good at doing.

1. If you are currently unemployed, use these ideas as a springboard to start earning an income once again.

2. If you already have a job, keep working at it and start your new business as a second job. As it develops and becomes profitable you have the option of making it your primary job.

BUSINESS STARTUP

Start your own business. Think it through, research it, test your idea, and run with it. Start in a physical location, online, or both. Do yourself a favor and invest as little money as possible when starting your business. If it succeeds, you can pour your money into it later on. If it fails, you haven't lost a bundle of money. Call upon the Lord for wisdom and leadership before doing anything.

Following are some potential business startup possibilities that would require minimal startup costs. This is only a starter list; there are hundreds of other possibilities, they include:

- income tax filing service
- home/office cleaning business
- window washing service, plant watering
- courier
- consignment shop
- grant writer
- wedding planner
- consultant to businesses in your field
- phone-calling service
- jewelry repair business
- videographer
- event coordinator
- private detective

- interior designer
- government consultant
- business coach
- travel consultant
- landscaper
- caterer
- add you own ideas…

ENTREPRENEURIAL

This is an area where you can apply your unique creative skills. A few starter ideas include:

- dust off and employ your current or past skills
- invent something
- consult in your area of entrepreneurship
- create a community newspaper or newsletter and sell advertising
- sell a friend's items on an online auction for a percentage of the sale
- researcher – medical, legal, humanitarian, historical, financial
- create a barter system…exchange your goods and/or services for theirs
- college professor / instructor
- TV producer/weather anchor
- add you own ideas…

HOME-BASED

There are hundreds of things you can do right out of your home. Consider opening your own home-based business. A few starter ideas include:

- delivery service
- baby-sitting service, an elderly-sitting service
- sell recyclable metals, plastic, newsprint
- pet sitting service

- bake brownies or cookies to sell to friends, at church, at work or at school
- help people with legal documents
- rake your neighbor's leaves or cut their grass for money
- delivery service for the elderly/homebound
- clean houses for pay
- add your own ideas…

MANAGERIAL

There managerial jobs available. You may have to have managerial experience to be hired in many of these fields. A few starter ideas include:
- manager in retail
- manager in an industrial company
- manager within any company within your areas of expertise
- manage a crew in a plant or factory
- healthcare provider manager
- property manager
- apartment manager
- facilities manager
- add your own ideas…

PROFESSIONAL

There are professional jobs available. You may have to have professional experience to be hired in many of these fields. A few starter ideas include:
- any professional job
- employment benefits counselor
- career in advertising
- public speaker
- teach at a community college or university
- write book reviews for newspapers/magazines
- substitute teacher
- put your coaching skills to use

- teach licensing courses
- banking consultant
- certified financial planner
- recruiter
- real estate appraiser
- occupational therapist
- graphic artist
- pharmacist
- stock broker
- legal consultant
- engineer
- accountant/CPA/tax consultant
- court reporter
- add your own ideas…

SALES

There are sales jobs available on the Internet and in most Sunday papers. Apply for one of them to gain experience to see how you like sales. A few samples listings include:
- inside or outside sales
- retail
- real estate
- sales representative
- auto parts store
- appliance store
- big box store
- electronics store
- add your own ideas…

SERVICE SECTOR

There are service sector jobs available. A few starter ideas include:
- any service job that appeals to you
- deliver newspapers
- deliver pizzas

- wash your neighbor's vehicles for a fee
- run errands for homebound people
- shovel someone's driveway – clear the snow
- laundry service for the elderly/homebound
- personal shopper for the elderly/homebound
- small appliance, automotive, lawn mower or boat repair service
- any service sector job you find a need to meet
- birthday party clown
- EMT/Firefighter
- weekend Nurse
- dental assistant
- administrative assistant
- weight loss consultant
- construction work
- alarm system installer
- telephone equipment installer
- cosmetologist
- barber
- driving instructor
- personal tutor
- guide
- stewardess
- security guard
- medical
- technical
- referee/umpire
- chef or short-order cook
- electronics
- gymnastics coach
- personal trainer
- image consultant
- add your own ideas…

Web-based

There are web-based jobs available. A few starter ideas include:
- web consultant

- create your own website
- become a web site designer
- information technician
- computer technician
- software technician
- computer networking
- data processing
- add your own ideas…

DEVELOP IDEAS OR LEADS OF YOUR OWN

Take these starter ideas and use them to springboard into a second career or business of your own. Again, call upon the Lord for wisdom and leadership before doing anything. May he bless you as you seek his will and seek to earn an income.

Did you see anything that appeals to you and matches your skills, abilities, and passion? If so it is time to have some fun dreaming about your future. God really does want to bless you. Review this verse from Chapter one: "For I know the plans I have for you, plans to prosper you and not to harm you, plans to give you hope and a future" Jeremiah 29:11. Ask God to lead you as you continue to reflect upon this list.

Many of these ideas could be applied rather quickly and with relative ease. Please do yourself a favor and be patient. When it comes to starting a business, don't get in a hurry. Many people who are experiencing financial distress may be tempted to follow an impulse to start their own business without the necessary planning and preparation. A word of caution: resist all urges to do that. Financial distress coupled with desperation can often lead to clouded thinking. Spend the necessary time thinking, talking, planning, and praying about your potential business startup. Talk about them with your family. Start slowly and with as little money as possible. You don't want to lose money. Just because something sounds good doesn't mean you should rush to start your own business.

If you choose to explore starting your own business, be careful. Resist the urge to enter in a dramatic fashion that could place both yourself and your family into shock and great financial risk. If you choose to explore starting your own business, approach it in a prayerful, methodical, deliberate and measured way and spare your family a lot of unnecessary grief. Please know that starting a business requires a lot of work and can be extremely exciting, rewarding, and even painful.

Home-based Business

If you choose to start your own business there is often no better place to begin than to start in your home. Many successful businesses started out in someone's basement or at someone's kitchen table. Some local zoning laws prohibit home-based businesses, so check with your local authorities before you start. There are many advantages to a home-based business: you already have an address, a phone, a computer, and a place for your office. You can ask your spouse and kids to help get things started and you can even pay them for their work.

Starting a home-based business can require very little up-front investment in cash. Most of the ideas on the lists require little or no money up front. If you choose one of them you don't run the risk of losing a lot of your hard-earned money. Be careful, because it is possible to spend several thousand dollars in startup costs that may never be recouped. Most small business ventures fail during their first year. They usually fail because of one or more of the reasons outlined in the next chapter.

Chapter 5
Taming the Business Failure Monster

There are some things you should consider before starting a business of your own. Some of the best lessons we can learn are lessons from the mistakes and failures made by other people. By learning from their mistakes you can avoid making those same costly mistakes should you decide to begin a new business of your own. New businesses have an unusually high rate of failure. The astounding thing is that many of the businesses that failed would have succeeded had their owner(s) done a few things differently.

10 Things That Practically Guarantee a Business Will Fail

1. Didn't have a well thought-through and highly-detailed business plan
2. Didn't do enough research into whether the business was needed and whether the product or service would sell
3. Didn't understand, grasp, and apply sound business principles
4. Didn't understand, or underestimated the competition
5. Didn't have the necessary knowledge or experience to start that particular business
6. Didn't have a realistic estimate of the total startup costs, or lacked startup funds
7. Didn't produce adequate cash flow once the business started
8. Didn't spend adequate time running the business in the beginning
9. Didn't start out small and grow larger, tried to start too big
10. Didn't allow for the multitude of hidden expenses required to operate a business

Should you choose to start your own home-based business do everything you possibly can to make it succeed. Study the ten reasons most businesses fail. Study it again and again, and avoid the pitfalls that cause businesses to fail.

Don't Pour Too Much Money into Your Business

Since we are in extraordinary financial times, wisdom suggests that you start slowly and with as little money invested as possible. All of the business opportunities on the list can be started in your home and do not require a separate location. There are great benefits to investing as little money as possible in a new business. One of the greatest benefits is that you are not subjecting yourself and your family to excessive financial risks.

Know When to Walk Away

One of the greatest benefits of not having a lot of money invested is this: it will be easier for you to let an unsuccessful business fail. If your business is not working and it doesn't appear that it has a realistic chance of succeeding, pull its plug and let it die. Resist the urge to keep pumping money into a leaky boat. At some point you have to back off, give it up, and move on to try something else. If you don't have a lot of money invested it will be much easier to walk away. On the other hand, if you have invested several thousand dollars in your business and you find that it is still not working, chances are very great that you will be reluctant to let it fail and try something different.

When Do I Invest a Lot of Money into My Business?

The short answer is: when your business begins to turn a consistent profit. Once you have hard evidence that your idea is working and your business is growing; that will be the right time to begin investing your hard-earned money. Be patient. Resist the urge to pump money into your business until you are sure that it is working and that it will continue to work into the future. You have a choice. You can either make your experience become one of your "best of times" or one of your "worst of times." If it becomes one of your best times you and your family will rejoice; on the other hand, if it becomes one of your worst times, you and your family will regret ever starting that business.

Finally, if you do start a business, be sure to check with your local authorities in order to set things up legally, and don't forget to pay your taxes. These actions can save money and prevent potential migraines later on.

Follow Proven Principles of Success

Your business or service will have a better chance of succeeding if you follow proven principles of success. If you apply these principles to your business venture you should begin to see growth relatively quickly and should begin making a profit within a reasonable length of time. Even the very best plans and actions incorporated into starting a business will have to undergo some modifications along the way. There is simply no way to anticipate everything that needs to be done, so expect to have to change a few things as you move forward. That doesn't indicate failure. It indicates that you have a normal business that needs some fine-tuning. If it doesn't grow and begin to make money you have a choice, you can either make the necessary adjustments to fine-tune your business, or you can choose to back off and try a different business opportunity.

22 Indicators That Accurately Predict a Potential Business' Success

1. Business plan

Develop a thoroughly detailed business plan that accurately states what you are attempting to do. It should be very specific and meticulous. It should cover every aspect of your new business idea.

2. Good match

Your new business must be a good match for who you are and the skills and abilities you possess. For example, should you be a person who detests selling a product or service, the last business you would want to start would be a sales-oriented business.

3. Experience and knowledge

You have either vast experience, knowledge or both in the type of business you plan to start. If you have no prior knowledge or experience in electrical engineering, why would you consider opening an electrical engineering company?

4. Good business skills

Employ good business skills coupled with hard work, dedication, and sacrifice. You have heard: "Work smarter, not harder." That is a valid principle, but so is the principle that hard work is unavoidable when starting a business.

5. More hard work

You are not just "talking" about working hard. You are actually committed to working very hard, up to 80 hours per week or more if necessary.

6. Research

Perform extensive research from every conceivable angle to determine market demand for products or services you plan to offer. If there is no need for another sporting goods store in your area, don't waste your time opening the 22nd store within a ten block area.

7. Demand

Choose your business based upon experience, knowledge, and positive product demand for your products or services. It might be hard to sell refrigerators in Antarctica or tanning beds in the Bahamas.

8. Location, location, location

Your product or service is something your vast knowledge or experience tells you are a good match for the area where you plan to do business. Will your customers be able to find your business? Will you advertise in the Yellow Pages? Will customers be able to access your location with relative ease? Of course, location is immaterial for home-based businesses.

9. Money

Determine the financial feasibility of starting your business. Ask yourself: "Can I really afford to do this without borrowing and putting myself and my family at great risk?"

10. Competition
You must know your competition. Answer these questions with all honesty: "Can I successfully enter the market and realistically expect to succeed while competing with the ABC Company?" "What goods or services will I provide that they can't?"

11. Expenses
List all possible expenses. Once you have listed everything, you will find that you may still have overlooked some unplanned expenses. List everything that comes to mind.

12. Marketing
Decide how you will market yourself, your business, and your products. Your services or products must be needed or is in great demand and should be able to be successfully marketed by you in today's economy.

13. Start-up money
Calculate how much start-up money it will take to begin and have more than that in hand before starting your business. There will be many hidden and unplanned expenses. For instance: taxes and licensing fees, just to name two.

14. Profitability
Your business should begin to make a profit. Remember, the object is to make money not to lose it. Making a profit is one of the best predictors that your business can succeed. However, simply making a profit is not enough. How you manage your profits and your business is a key component.

15. Management
Great businesses succeed because of great management. Management skills are inherent for some, but they may also be acquired. Even a bad business can be managed in such a way as to make it profitable. Likewise, a great business can be managed in such a way that it will fail. Good management is a great indicator that a business will succeed.

16. Timing
Timing is crucial and many underestimate this concept. Is this the right time to start my business or would I be better off waiting six months or a year before starting?

17. Legal protection
It would be wise for you to both incorporate and insure your business. These can protect your other assets from legal judgments should unforeseen problems arise. Do your own research with local experts concerning these matters.

18. Patience
Most business doesn't start off with a bang. Start small and do everything you can to insure steady growth. Start small and be patient.

19. Trust
If you are unethical with yourself, your employees, your suppliers, and your customers, you should expect to have nothing but perpetual problems. You have to be honest and above-board in everything you do.

20. Your Word
Keep your word. If you say you will do something…do it. Don't get in a habit of having to make excuses.

21. Fairness
Be fair to your employees and customers. The first hint they pick up on the fact that you are being unfair, they will make you pay for it.

22. Integrity
Operate every aspect of your business, and make every business decision in ways that would always glorify God and be pleasing to him. If you do this, you both lessen your potential problems, and increase your chances of success exponentially.

THE MAN WHO MADE GOD HIS BUSINESS PARTNER
R. G. Letourneau was a committed Christian who made God his business partner. Often referring to God as the chairman of the board, this Stockton, California native used his God-given abilities to design,

develop, and produce heavy earth-moving equipment. His machines were first used in farming, but with the onset of World War II he won contracts with the U.S. Army. His equipment had become so advanced that he produced more than two thirds of all the Army's earth-moving equipment during the war. God blessed Letourneau's partnership with him immensely. Letourneau became very wealthy. God blessed him so much financially that he began giving God more and more of his income. He reached such unparalleled success in business that every year he gave God 90% of all his earnings and lived off the remaining 10%. R. G. Letourneau demonstrated the awesome fact that God honors people who will trust and obey his will for their lives.

Get Excited about Your Future

With God's help and your hard work, these may have the potential to become some of the best of times in life for you and your family. Granted, you may be unemployed and you may feel that there are no realistic job possibilities in sight. God sometimes works in strange ways. You may lose your job and find a better one. You may lose your job and be unable to find another for an extended period of time. Trusting God with your career may be the hardest thing you have ever attempted. It can also be a time for unprecedented character development and spiritual growth.

A major accomplishment you can make to allow you to show your money who's boss and tame the money monster is that of gaining control of your career. Your skills and abilities produce income. Income allows you to provide for yourself and your family. Get excited about your future and trust in the Lord. This may be one of the greatest opportunities to trust God and grow in your faith that you will ever have. Engage in activities that will position you for a successful job search or business start-up. The very best days of your life may lie just ahead.

Next, we will be looking at a critical subject in this crazy economy…how you can layoff proof your job.

Chapter 6
Taming the Layoff Monster

There are immediate steps you can take that can help you layoff proof your job. By taking deliberate steps to layoff proof your job, you will have accomplished one of the most important steps toward showing your money who's boss and taming the money monster of layoffs because you will have taken decisive steps to lock-in a stable income. With several million people desperate for jobs you may choose to do everything in your power to protect the job you have. A friend works in a big box store where 20-30 people a day sit at a kiosk and enter computerized applications for employment. What the hopeful applicants don't know is that the store where they are applying has already begun its second round layoffs of part-time employees. In addition, they have begun cutting hours of full timers, and are facing even tougher choices should sales continue to lag. Many companies have instituted hiring freezes and have cut back to a bare-bones level of employment in order to secure their company's futures. Many owners of small businesses have followed suit. Don't be too offended, for if you owned your own business you would probably be doing exactly the same thing. Some of the business owners who are reading this book have had to make those tough decisions and have laid off people who used to work for them. As one looks at the reality of today's economic situation the sad truth is very harsh.

YOU MAY LOSE YOUR JOB

This will be a 100% unavoidable fact for millions of people. In late 2008 and early 2009, layoffs already exceeded 540,000 at America's 500 largest companies. This number doesn't include the hundreds of thousands of layoffs from smaller companies and businesses across America. Some businesses and companies have failed and others will fail. If you are one of the unfortunate ones who lose their job, you may simply be a victim of your company's scaling back or their demise. Bad things happen, they are nobody's fault, they just happen. Resist the temptation to become angry with your boss or your company. Don't take it personally; your boss is just following orders laid down by his boss, who in turn may have been given those orders by an even higher boss. Get the picture. It could have nothing to do with you at all. Considering the economic climate of the U.S., layoffs could be a matter of survival for your former company. This fact doesn't lessen the pain. You will definitely miss the money because your living expenses are ongoing and your bills will continue to come in even though you are not employed.

Unwritten Lists for Job Layoffs

When bosses begin the arduous task of deciding who they must lay off they usually follow a process. This process follows sets of written and unwritten rules. While there are no guarantees, there are some things you can do to insure that you will not be the first person who comes to mind when your boss gets ready to start laying off or firing employees. A great many bosses consult a specific list of people when it is time to begin layoffs. Your boss is very familiar with this list; in fact, he keeps his list with him 100% of the time. He never leaves home or work without it. He always takes his list when he is with his family at a restaurant, shopping, or at the movies. His list accompanies him when he is running, playing tennis, or golfing. He keeps his list with him when he goes on vacation, when he works in the yard, when he showers, and even when he sleeps. You ask: "Where does he keep his list, and why have I have never seen it?" You may be surprised to know that at this stage of the layoff process, his list is unwritten. It is a "mental list," that exists only in your boss's mind.

Believe me; you don't want your name on your boss's mental list. If a layoff is considered or needed, he begins creating his layoff list by drawing from the pool of employees' names he has in his mind. The names he selects are the names of the people he thinks the company could do without. At that point in the process the last name you want to have included on his mental layoff list is your name. When he begins putting names on paper, it is time to lay people off.

Attitudes and Actions that can Cost You your Job

In the following pages you will find descriptions of workers common to most workplaces. You will recognize some of the people you work alongside every day. Depending upon how your company or boss sees things, your involvement in any one of them or any combination of them may cause you to be added to your boss's layoff list. At the same time, avoiding any one of them or any combination of them may prevent your name from even being considered for a layoff. These caricatures describe various types of problematic employees. The three things that qualify them as problematic employees are their thinking, their decision making, and their behavior. You will have no problem envisioning many people you work alongside on a daily basis. A few may even cheer and take delight in the fact that some are getting a small dose of what they deserve because someone is finally exposing them. Experience will confirm that these practices actually do result in layoffs and terminations.

Will you see Yourself on the List?

As you examine the following caricatures, please consider the most difficult, emotional, and most personal part of the equation. Consider for a moment that the fait accompli or self-evident truth is the fact that your thinking, your decision making, or your behavior could be causing problems with other people where you work, including your boss. Some of the faces you see may be the faces you are making as you look into the mirror and see yourself and your own behavior. However, any anger, frustration, discomfort, or emotional pain that you may experience will be worth it. Why, because if you really want to layoff proof yourself and your job, you will have to face the realities of what type of employee you are.

Learn to Laugh at Yourself

Among the hardest things for me and you to see are our own faults, flaws, mistakes, and sins. Like me, every reader will be tempted to see everyone else but himself or herself in the following descriptions. Your natural reaction will be that of wanting to laugh at some of the people you work with when you see them described in the following pages. Laughing at someone else is fun; we do it all the time.

But notice that I started with laughter first being directed at oneself. One of the greatest gifts anyone can have is that of not taking himself or herself too seriously. If you can laugh at yourself when you mess up or when someone tells a joke at your expense, people will have much more respect for you than if you get mad and sulk. Seeing you getting mad actually makes them laugh at you more than they would have.

Have a little fun as you read the caricatures. They represent real people that I have either worked for, have worked alongside, or who have worked for me. Have some fun reading the list. Various people you know will come to mind. Share this list with some of your friends at work and enjoy a laugh or two. But be sure to have a good laugh or two at your own expense as well. As you read them you will likely see yourself in more of these caricatures than you may want to admit.

BOSS' MASTER LIST OF PEOPLE TARGETED FOR LAYOFFS

1. **The Newbie**: "The last to be hired is the first to be fired." You need to know that your layoff is not your fault. It is nothing but an economic and timing issue.

2. **The Slacker**: "Workers who are nonproductive are out the door." If you are not making a contribution to your company or business in some significant way, you may be in line for a layoff or termination. Quit goofing off and make a to-do list every morning.

3. **The Baby**: "Everyone is really getting tired of babysitting him." Babies are great, but not at work. Become a self-starter. Make a goal of having never to be told what work to do next. Take charge of your job and give it your very best effort.

4. **Mr. Incompetent**: "He either can't or is not doing his job." Your inability to do your job may be a result of being undisciplined or lacking skills or motivation. Spend some significant time mapping a strategy to gain control of your job.

5. **The Whiner**: "She's a whiner on a mission…a perpetual pity party." Many people get wrapped up in their own personal pity parties. Grow up. People are sick of your constant whining. Try going a full 30 minutes without whining. After you can do that than make it an hour and then two hours. Put yourself through basic training.

6. **The Manipulator**: "He does nothing but manipulate our other employees." You are a champion at self-centeredness. Start doing your

own work and quit attempting to "play" everyone else. The last laugh may be on you because you may be the object of your fellow employees' manipulation and not even know it. Stop manipulating everyone else and start being honest and above board in your dealings with others.

7. **The Gripe Machine**: "All she ever does is constantly complain about everything. I have nicknamed her 'The Gripe Machine.'" People are sick and tired of hearing your constant gripes. Learn to leave your negativity and complaining in the car on the way to and from work. For a change, commit to giving 10 compliments every day.

8. **The Spoon**: "He can't get along with other employees: all he ever does is to stir things up or keep them stirred up." Look for positive ways to redirect your energies and attitudes to accomplish positive results for the company and your fellow employees.

9. **Mr. Negative**: "He has nothing to offer but a negative attitude." People are sick of your negativity. Learn to keep your negative comments to yourself. For a change, surprise everyone and say 10 positive things every day.

10. **Ms. Undependable**: "She is just not a dependable employee." You had better get your act together because you are on the boss's list. Start by being on time and then begin showing some initiative by doing your job in a way that would cause your boss to want to compliment your performance.

11. **Sneaky Snake**: "He is so untrustworthy and sneaky." People do not trust you. Write out a list of five things you can do to earn the trust of the people you work with.

12. **Sticky Fingers**: "He's always stealing from the company: money, time, or materials." Do you steal property or people's reputations? You must stop immediately. Go cold-turkey; don't steal anything for a full day, then two days, and so on…

13. **The Liar**: "The only thing I can say about her is that she's a liar." No one trusts you to tell the truth about anything. They figure that if you will lie about the little things you will lie about anything. The quick-fix is…always tell the truth.

14. **The Sexual Harasser**: "Has the guy never heard of sexual harassment charges?" You probably need professional counseling. Seek

help immediately and learn to keep your hands and words to yourself. This can get you fired more quickly than you think.

15. **Potty Mouth**: "His words are an indicator of his substandard vocabulary." The vocabulary you choose to use says a lot about you. Quick way to stop…pay a coworker five dollars each time you use a four-letter word. A couple of $50 days will cause you to clean up your language very quickly.

16. **Ms. Unreliable**: "She really doesn't want to work: she is always late, leaving early, or asking off." You are better than this. Write out 10 things that you can begin doing today that will change peoples' perception of you.

17. **The Surfer**: "We are paying him to work, not to surf." Do your surfing on your own time. You are being paid to work, not to check your email and favorite web sites. Turn off your ISP and use that time helping another employee with a project or two.

18. **Mr. Break Room Manager**: "He always hangs out in the break room. 'Where's Bill, let me guess…?'" This is not the type of reputation to be sought after. Begin pulling your part of the load because people resent your having too much free time.

19. **Ms. Socialite: the MIA**: "She can never be found when you need her." If your boss knew how much time you spend getting out of work you would be fired. People resent your attitude and actions. Stay at your workplace. If you have to leave, tell someone where you are going, and be back ASAP.

20. **Lazy Susan**: "She never pulls her weight around the workplace." You are on your boss's list. Starting today, you need to start pulling your weight. In fact, do something different and actually do more than is expected of you. You will turn heads.

21. **The Mirage**: "He only works when he sees me coming." People resent your behavior. Your boss may not be as oblivious to your actions as you think. Play a trick on your coworkers and begin working hard all the time, not just when the boss comes around. Who knows, you might even get a raise.

22. **Ms. Two-Faced**: "She says one thing to my face and another behind my back." There is one thing you have going for you…everyone lacks respect for you. You can change and better yourself if you

will start building people up instead of tearing them down. Learn to treat people the way you want to be treated.

23. **The Tattler**: "You should have heard her the other day. 'Hey boss, do you know what Stacey just…'" People, including your boss, despise your actions. You are acting like a four-year-old. Grow up, stop tattling, and get a life. When you stop this destructive behavior, people might actually be friends with you again. The next time you are tempted to tattle, go tattle to the boss on yourself.

24. **The Judge**: "She thinks she works here to judge everyone." Stop thinking you are perfect. The faster you stop this nonsense the better off you and everyone else will be. Come down off your throne and live among the humans once again, you may find that even they are fun to be around most of the time.

25. **The Jury**: "Don't confuse him with the facts; his mind is already made up about everything." The only court you are in is called kangaroo. Why do you find everyone else guilty? Stop worrying about everyone else and concentrate on cleaning up your own act. People may begin to warm up to you if you will cut them a little slack.

26. **The Executioner**: "The guy is ruthless in the way he treats other people." Stop stabbing people in the back. That is no way to win friends. You need to win the trust of the people you work with and the only way to do that is to start treating people fairly. Jesus said something about doing unto others: "So in everything, do to others what you would have them do to you…" Matthew 7:12.

27. **Mr. Universe**: "He is the most inconsiderate person I have ever had work for me." It may come as a big surprise, but there are a few other people in this world besides you. Begin treating people with respect and as valued members of the human race and you will go places.

28. **Mr. Superiority**: "He never helps out with other people's projects: he thinks he's just too good for everyone else." Do you really think you are better than everyone else or do you just come across that way? You either need a good dose of humility or some image enhancement. Roll up your sleeves and start helping out.

29. **The Text Berry**: "All I ever get is a busy signal. She takes her phone off the hook and spends most of her time on her text berry."

Leave the thing at home or in your car. Throw it away, smash it, it doesn't matter what you do; just put it where it can't get you in trouble at work. Use all your new-found time to apply yourself to your job. You may get a surprise in the form of a raise.

30. **Ms. Gossip**: "She's the owner of the gossip and rumor mills around here." If you can't say something good about a person, don't say anything at all. Surprise your coworkers and stop cold-turkey. Replace your gossip with positive words of encouragement. You may surprise everyone and become one of the most popular persons at work.

31. **The Favor Granter:** "All I ever hear about her is that she provides 'favors' to some of the guys from the office, and he is the go-to guy if someone wants to buy drugs at work." Stop these types of behavior immediately, because these are the quickest ways to have your termination or layoff ticket punched. Regain your self-respect and commit yourself to making something happen with your genuine work-related skills.

32. **Mr. Contraband**: "The guy is always on the borderline of being illegal." This behavior covers all types of illegal behaviors, substances, offensive materials, workplace violence, or weapons. These activities can get your lay off ticket punched, paint a target on your back, or can land you in jail. The answer to this is to stop.

33. **Mr. Put-Down**: "You wouldn't believe what that guy said to me a couple of years ago." A sound practice is that of being judicious in what you say to everyone where you work. Once spoken, your words cannot be recalled; you never know when your words may come back to hurt you.

The behaviors or practices of any of these 33 caricatures could cause you to lose your job. No doubt, there are others as well. When a subjective boss begins writing down the names of the people he wants to lay off, if you fit any one or any combination of these descriptions, you may be added to his layoff list. At the same time, NOT DOING some of them or any combination of them may prevent your name from even being considered as an addition to his list.

Do you Want to Layoff Proof Yourself and Your Job?

If you answered yes, I have one more question. How badly do you want to reach that goal? If you are waiting for someone else, or for a certain set of circumstances to come along and make you layoff proof, you are wasting your time. The only way you will ever enjoy a high degree of job security is for you to take charge of your life, your job, and your personal work-ethic. One of the principles of success in the workplace is that you are in charge of your performance as an employee. Now is the time for you to step up to the plate and take charge of yourself, your job, your performance, your attitude, your behavior, your work-ethic, and your career. Only you can layoff proof yourself and your job. Are you ready to step up and get on with the rest of your life?

There are No Guarantees but Your Chances are Good

Understand that there is no guarantee that if you eliminate these issues you will keep your job. While they are no guarantees, your chances are greatly improved. If you will follow the proven results-oriented principles that have worked for millions of people through the ages, you can layoff proof yourself. We will consider them in greater detail in a moment.

Common sense dictates that there are many things you can do to insure that you will NOT be among the first persons who come to mind when your boss gets ready to start laying off or firing employees. With hard work and creativity you can insure that your name is placed on your boss's "preferred" list. This is your boss's "good" mental list. It is the list of people he or she wishes to keep as employees no matter what the cost.

Do the Exact OPPOSITE of These 33 Things

And the list goes on. You get the picture. You can virtually layoff proof your job by doing just the opposite of these 33 things. If you have been doing any of these things then…STOP…doing them immediately. Stopping may be tough, but it may just save you your job. This may also be tough because most of us are myopic when it comes to seeing our own faults. Examine your specific job situation to find how many other rules that would apply to your job specifically. An experienced military person once said: "When standing in formation, don't do anything that would get you noticed." To keep your job: don't get yourself noticed doing any of the 33 things listed above.

Be Painfully Honest

Which of the above need your immediate attention as they relate to your job? Pick out the top one or two and make the appropriate changes immediately. After those issues are resolved, work on the next one and so on. To see ourselves as others see us…you will need to have thick skin, but you may wish to consider asking a close friend at work to look at the list and give an honest critique of your work behavior and performance. Whether you chose to make improvements yourself or ask a friend for help, make the changes you need to make. The job you save may be your own.

The Key is to Do Something…Starting Today!

My second book, **Layoff Proof Your Job:** *Cracking the Layoff Code* is based upon the 33 caricatures you just read. It takes a much deeper look into how one successfully layoff proofs oneself and one's job. It is available at Amazon.com.

Chapter 7
Taming the Termination Monster

Steps to Help you Keep Your Job

There are several definite steps you may take that will help you gain the positive recognition you deserve while helping you keep your job. Again, there are no guarantees, but these things may help you lay-off proof your job and prevent you from being terminated. By engaging in the 25 principles listed below, you may increase your chances of keeping your job if or when the layoffs begin in your company.

1. Work harder AND work smarter.
2. Make yourself valuable to your company.
3. Work at getting along with your boss and everyone else.
4. Play by company rules.
5. Volunteer for extra or tough assignments.
6. Arrive for work early.
7. Be the first to volunteer to work overtime if asked to finish a project.
8. Learn new computer or other unique skills that no one else has.
9. Keep a private log of your accomplishments. (Never show these to anyone except your boss, and then, only if it is needed…use your own better judgment here.)
10. Give a full day's work for a full day's pay.
11. Be loyal to your company for as long as you work there.
12. Be honest and above reproach.
13. Be easily approachable.
14. Really know your stuff, gain a mastery over your assigned job.
15. Always make your boss look good.
16. Keep your cool in all situations, be a person of balance.
17. Never be afraid to give honest compliments.

18. Be an exemplary employee and work well with other people.
19. Don't criticize other workers or management.
20. Refuse to be a whiner.
21. Never put another person down.
22. Watch what you say to and about other people.
23. Don't agree with other people when they are belittling someone.
24. Never stab another person in the back.
25. Always remember, it's never wrong to do the right thing.

On and on it goes. You get the picture. You can virtually layoff proof or terminate proof your job by engaging in these 25 principles. If you have been or are still doing any of them, CONTINUE doing them and any others you wish to implement.

It may come as a surprise for some, it may burst the bubbles of a few others, and it will really wreak havoc with those who have been educated in the "self-esteem" based educational system of many of today's public schools. But, here it is anyway…

Your Job is a Privilege, Not a Right

Again, it may come as a surprise to you, but your boss does not have to let you work for him or for his company. You have been extended the opportunity to work there because you possess a skill set, knowledge, or an ability that is valuable to that business or company. Unfortunately, if you come to the place where you no longer benefit the company, you will no longer be needed…it's that simple. If you become less productive and someone comes along who can do more for your company than you, you may be out of a job. Look at the way professional sports teams treat their former stars and legends of past seasons. They trade them. Not many employees hang around for long beyond their usefulness to the company. This is not to suggest that you should become paranoid about your job; that will only make you miserable. However, avoid having the "I'm God's gift to this company," attitude. No one likes arrogance and that type of pride. Not your fellow employees, your supervisor, your boss, the CEO, and not even God himself likes arrogance and improper pride. The scriptures say: "There are six things the LORD hates, seven that are detestable to him: haughty eyes, a lying tongue, hands that shed innocent blood, a heart that devises wicked schemes, feet that are quick to rush into evil, a false witness who pours out lies and a man who stirs up dissension among brothers" Proverbs 6:16-19. Translated to the workplace it means. "The boss hates: arrogance, a liar, a troublemaker, someone who is always plotting evil, someone who is always quick to do evil, someone who lies to get others in trouble, and a person who is himself a troublemaker."

I Have Already Lost my Job, Now What Do I Do?

Don't take it Personally

If you have lost your job it may have nothing to do with you personally. In this tough economy companies are forced to choose to take drastic steps for their own financial survival. Layoffs and terminations happen: with money tight and consumer spending down, some companies have no choice but to begin laying off or terminating some of their workforce. The first round of layoffs usually affects the newest, the part-time, or the most unproductive employees. In an attempt to maintain the company's survivability, the second round usually trims the workforce even more. If your company survives long enough to implement a third or fourth wave, they are probably attempting to avoid either going out of business or bankruptcy. Remember, they are doing this in order to survive. Wise business owners and companies will do whatever it takes to survive. If a companies' survival depends upon laying off 40% of its workforce in order to stay in business its owner has no choice but to lay them off. Business owners aren't necessarily cruel people who enjoy seeing their workforce reduced, but if survival means laying off 40% of their employees they have to make that call no matter whom it hurts. The fortunate ones are the other 60% who remain employed. However, some companies are either so deeply in debt, or are unable to continue selling their goods or services that they will ultimately have to close their doors forever.

Unfortunately, the stark reality for some is that you find yourself unemployed and you may not be able to find a job because of the vast numbers of other people are also out of work and looking for jobs. If you do feel that you did something that contributed to your layoff there are some things you can do to change your situation. Here are a few positive steps you can take that will enable you to survive financially and find another job one day.

DEVELOP PERSONAL ACTION PLANS
1. Talk to your HR department and sign up for unemployment.
2. Review the lists in previous chapters for ideas about how to earn money while you are between jobs. Or, use the ideas to launch a new career.
3. Seek financial assistance from your church, government programs, private sources, family, or friends. Ask for a handout. Resist the urge to borrow money from a friend or family member, because you will most likely see the relationship change from friend to that of debtor. Keep your friendships viable. Don't ask to borrow money…you may be unable to pay it back.
4. Cut back on ALL necessary expenditures.
5. Eliminate ALL optional spending.
6. Contact ALL of your creditors and tell them what happened. Ask them to work with you by allowing you to make small minimum payments.
7. Begin looking for work. Be honest with yourself and your family…it could take a while to find a job. Don't give up on your job search. Apply to scores of places.
8. Use this time to BETTER yourself and your family NOT to EMBITTER them.
9. Don't beat yourself up. Know that things will get better someday. Thousands have been in similar circumstances as you and survived. You can survive as well.
10. Draw closer to the Lord. He is on your side and wants to help you. Pray and study God's Word every day. Get involved in a good church and build relationships with people there.

MAINTAIN A POSITIVE ATTITUDE
Your family is looking to your for leadership. You can set the tone for how the family deals with the financial crisis you are experiencing. You can provide the leadership needed to lead them back to the Lord. Keep going to church or find a friendly Bible-believing church and start attending next Sunday. The Lord and his people can offer friendship,

acceptance, moral support, prayers, and many other things. You may never know what God will do unless you put yourself in a position to receive his blessings. Finally, be honest and realistic with yourself and your family. Things may get worse before they get better. Expect the best, but prepare for the worst. Millions of Americans need jobs.

BE WILLING TO WORK AT ANYTHING THAT IS NOT ILLEGAL, IMMORAL, OR SINFUL.

Find work that doesn't violate either God's laws or man's. Drug dealing, prostitution, pornography, the abortion industry, and many other things are out of the question. Any job that deliberately brings harm to yourself or another person would be unacceptable. Be willing to work at anything that is not illegal, immoral, or sinful. Because of our economic times you may have to work far beneath your skill level, below your training, and even further below what you think you deserve. But you will survive.

I know a man who worked an assistant manager at a retail store that employed 125 people. Each night when it was his turn to close, he cleaned all the restrooms. He did this in order to remind himself that he was no better than anyone else in the company, and to set an example for others to follow. Needless to say, he had the respect of everyone who worked there. His hard work, leadership skills, and attitude paid off as he has since been promoted to store manager. Are you willing to humble yourself to do things like that?

You have the opportunity to distinguish yourself from all the other job applicants in your area when entering into your job search. One of the best ways you can distinguish yourself is to follow this principle. Most people refuse to do menial labor-related jobs...like construction, housecleaning, making beds and cleaning toilets in motel rooms, or landscaping. In times like these, that may be the only job you can find. Most of them may already be taken. If that is the only job you can find, would anyone in their right mind blame you for taking it? That job might save your home, your family, and might just allow you to survive your financial crisis. Sure, there are much better jobs out there so go for them first, but don't be too good to do the menial labor if that's what it comes down to. Businessmen are all the time saying that they just can't find anyone who wants to work. Often, when they do find someone willing to work, that person is not always qualified...they either lack some of the necessary skills, or they can't pass the drug test. If you are doing drugs now you need to STOP if you want to get a job.

EXTRAORDINARY TIMES REQUIRE EXTRAORDINARY MEASURES IN RESPONSE.
Everyone would like to have a high paying job with lots of prestige and great benefits. There are a lot of jobs out there that are like this. If you sit back and refuse to work until you have one of those plumb jobs you may suddenly wake up one day ten years from now and find that you haven't worked for ten years. You have to start somewhere. Earning $8 per hour is far better than earning zero dollars per hour and earning $30,000 per year is far better than earning zero thousand per year. Go ahead and take the $8 per hour job while you are looking for the $50.00 per hour job. Work for a company that pays $30,000 per year while searching for the $150,000 per year job. At least you will be bringing in some much needed income.

BE CREATIVE
There are definite steps you may begin taking today that can help you layoff-proof and terminate proof your job. You are the only one who can take those steps. Do something to distinguish yourself from the others you work with. Your boss will definitely take notice. When he asks you why you are different, be sure and have a good answer ready to give him. Consider the ideas you have read, use the ones that would benefit you, and come up with other strategies of your own.

Again, the Key is to Do Something…Starting Today!

Chapter 8
Taming The Budget Busters Monsters

FINANCIAL ADHD

Attention-Deficit Hyperactivity Disorder (ADHD) affects approximately 5% of the U.S. population. Its primary symptoms include: inattention, impulsiveness, and hyperactivity.

When it comes to personal money management many people experience a type of Financial ADHD. Financial ADHD is experienced by a far greater percentage of the American adult population than medical ADHD. To be clear, Financial ADHD is not a medical disorder. It is my descriptive term for the millions of Americans who exhibit the symptoms of inattention, impulsiveness, or hyperactivity when it comes to their finances and spending practices. That millions of Americans exhibit these symptoms relative to their finances, spending practices, and credit card abuse is obvious. When one looks at the levels of personal debt and credit card abuse one sees an ugly picture.

People spend inattentively, impulsively, and hyperactively. Why all this irrational spending and where did it come from? Most people are bombarded with spending opportunities every day. You can hardly go anywhere without having an ATM machine available. If you listen closely, you can almost hear them calling your name. They are like the Sirens in Homer's Odyssey singing the beautiful notes, begging you to withdraw and spend some money. The latest technology now allows manufacturers to imbed sensors in some of the products we drive, wear, and carry so that we can be targeted with advertisements on our phones, IPods, signs, or on some high-tech billboards.

We have witnessed the proliferation of cable shopping channels, infomercials, telemarketing calls, and gazillions of computer pop-up ads. Millions are now receiving ads on their cell phones by text messages. The average one hour television program has a full 20 minutes of commercials strongly urging you to buy their products. Billboards are everywhere and advertising is on our busses, trains, taxis, airplanes, menus, and even in restrooms. The average magazine contains more advertising than articles or news stories. The same is true of newspapers and the Internet is an advertiser's goldmine. People fighting for your dollars have reached a fever pitch and are out of control. With all these spending opportunities relentlessly bombarding all of us, one can see why we are a nation with uncontrollable debt and out-of-control spending.

For some, the cure may be very easy and almost effortless. For others, it will be one of the toughest journeys you have ever taken. For all, it will have to be an intentional and deliberate decision to show your money who's boss, defeat the money monster of impulsive spending, and gaining control of your finances. Something this significant will not happen accidentally.

1. Inattention

Start Paying Attention

Many people have no idea how much money they spend when they are not paying attention. They frequently run out of money and wonder where it all went. They just don't pay attention. For example: how many people do you know who never balance their checkbooks? They constantly stop by the ATM, go online, or call their bank to check on their available balance. They are the people who don't know where their money goes. If you listen closely you will hear someone say these very words: "I just don't know where all my money goes."

On the other extreme, some people fastidiously document every single penny they spend. This behavior or over-attention to finances is not necessary. It can be weird. That is fine if that is for you, but this book is not advocating that type of extreme behavior. It is advocating a balanced approach. You need know how much money you have, and then exercise control over your spending. Controlling your spending is far better than allowing your spending to control you.

Watch Out for Pick-Pockets

Your money is your money. It does not belong to someone else. If you don't control it someone else will. Unfortunately, you may be having your pockets picked every day. This is not being done by professional pick pockets, but by highly motivated salesmen, retail stores, TV shopping clubs, the Internet, and others. It is your money. If it is going to be controlled, it will be YOU who has to control it. You have the ability to take charge of your money. P. T. Barnum, of Barnum and Bailey Circus fame, once had an insightful saying about a fool and his money being soon parted. Don't be foolish with your money. Learn sound principles about how to control your money and make it work for you. There are potentially hundreds of people vying for your money. Since they all want some of your money, you will gain the advantage over them by developing a spending plan to help you make good spending decisions and help you develop good spending habits. If you don't have a good grip on your money, you will lose it. Thank God for the following poignant truth from Scripture: "Do not conform any longer to the pattern of this world, but be transformed by the renewing of your mind. Then you will be able to test and approve what God's will is—his good pleasing and perfect will" Romans 12:2.

Beware of Hidden Budget Busters

Let's examine some examples of inattention to spending. These examples will give you an idea where a lot of your money could be going. They are hidden budget busters because, for the most part, these are hidden expenses that most people never consider.

Watching Your Money Go up in Smoke

Buying two packs of cigarettes per day at an average cost of $4.00 per pack equals $56.00 a week for one person or $112.00 per week for two people. Multiply that by 52 weeks and one person spends $2,912.00 per year, and two people spend $5,824.00 per year. Over a ten year period that equals: $29,120.00 for one person and $58,240.00 for two people. Over a forty year period that equals: $116,480.00 for one person and $232,960.00 for two people. How much money would you have if you saved and invested that amount each year and left it to grow over 40 years in a tax-free Roth IRA? Smoking secession will have a massive impact on your finances, and a positive impact upon your health as well.

SPENDING CAN BE INTOXICATING

Consider the impact that alcohol can have on your budget. Consuming two $15 bottles of wine at home, or six $5.00 beers or mixed drinks in a bar per week equals $30.00 per week, or $1,560 per year. Over a period of ten years it would equal $15,600. Over a forty year period it would equal $62,400. And that is just for one person. If two people in the family drink that amount each day the figures equal more than $3,000 per year and more than $31,000 over a ten year period. In forty years you will have drunk the equivalent of a $120,000 IRA. That's not chump change. How much money would you have if you saved and invested that amount each year and left it to grow over 40 years in a tax-free Roth IRA?

WHERE'S THE BEEF?

Clara Peller was a darling little lady who popularized the phrase: "Where's the Beef?" for a popular fast food chain's commercials during the 1980s. Just how much is that fast food costing you per week, per year, or over a lifetime? Everyone wants to eat out sometimes. It's fun, it's convenient, and it sometimes tastes pretty good too. A mere $20 per week amounts to $1,040 per year. That totals more than $40,000 over a 40 year period. If your family spends $100 per week in restaurants that total comes to $5,200 per year, or more than $200,000 over a 40 year period. How much money would you have if you saved and invested that amount each year and left it to grow over 40 years in a tax-free Roth IRA? No one is against eating out. Everyone needs a break from cooking and there are times when your time is more valuable than the price of the meal. Eating out is great so long as you know where your money is going and that you can afford it. But, be sure and watch out for the massive amounts of calories and fat inherent in most fast foods, for they can bring on other problems.

GOURMET COFFEE

At $4-$5 per cup, you can spend a fortune a year on those great tasting hot beverages many like to enjoy. I recently heard of one couple who were spending $275.00 per month on their favorite gourmet coffees. They were enjoying the delicious beverages, but decided that they could spend the money on more important things than coffee. Do the math: one per work day totals $1,000-$1,250 per year. That totals more than $40,000 over a period of 40 years.

OTHER HIDDEN BUDGET BUSTERS

You can find other Budget Busters of your own, but consider these: CDs, DVDs, Internet downloads, text messaging, lottery tickets, convenience store snacks, clothing, and many others you can add to the list. Stop. You are taking all my vices away. No, you are adding money to your own pockets. A mere $20 per week spent on CDs, DVDs, or lottery tickets equal more than $1,000 per year or $40,000 over a 40 year period.

2. IMPULSIVENESS

Impulse spending means that you are making excessive unplanned purchases. An example of impulse spending that we can identify with is a trip to the gas station. You stop by the station, and while pumping gas you see a display of your favorite sodas and candy bars so you decide to get one of each. Zappo, you go inside, buy one of each and drive off into the sunset eating candy and drinking soda. That is an example of innocent impulsive spending. You spent three bucks and got a sugar and caffeine jolt. Now, you don't do this every time you stop for gas do you? Well…yes, some do, but most of us don't. If you buy those items every time you stop for gas it is not impulse spending, it is a habit.

Sometimes impulse spending can be a good thing. You are on your way home from work and you are thinking about what a wonderful wife or husband you have. You feel so blessed and are thanking the Lord for them as you drive. Then it hits you. Stop and buy her some flowers, or him a box of brownies at your local supermarket. You stop, make your purchase, and then surprise them with a blessing when you walk in the door. You were impulsive, but you could afford it and it sure was fun. It was a really good thing to do for your spouse. The key concept here is having the maturity and self-control to know when to say no to your impulses.

Remember my friend who was listening to his car radio and heard that he could get a free cooler by stopping by a certain car dealership. All he had to do was test drive a new car. He and his wife loaded the kids up in their car, hurried over to the car dealership, took their test drive, and you guessed it…he proudly accepted ownership of his "free" cooler for which he paid $25,000. Now, that is impulse spending. In 2008 a TV news story highlighted a car dealer who was offering a deal where customers would get a specific brand new car for the sum of $1.00 when they bought any other new car from him at the full sticker price. That was a great deal for those who needed two new cars at once and could afford to pay for them, their taxes, and insurance. One has to wonder how many people went impulsive on that opportunity.

Watch out for Impulsive Spending

This is a really tough one because we have all been trained to spend impulsively by our culture. Look at the way various items are arranged on the shelves in any retail store. They are practically jumping off the shelves at you. ALL of the items beside the checkout stands are impulsive spending, high margin items. It is no accident that they are right there beside the cash register. They are placed there by design. In essence, your favorite retailer is trying to squeeze every last penny out of your pocket when you check out. We should resent it, for they are trying to pick our pockets and take our dollars away from us a few at a time.

Cures for the Impulsive Shopper

- Never allow yourself to go shopping alone
- Never take a credit card with you when you shop
- Always pay with cash only when you shop
- Limit the amount of cash you take with you when shopping
- Write out and take a shopping list with you
- Strictly stick to your list

EXTREME CURES
- Cut up your credit cards
- Cut your cable or satellite service to avoid shopping channels, infomercials
- Sell or give away your computer to stop shopping abuse

"...I will put my laws in their minds, and write them on their hearts. I will be their God, and they will be my people..." Hebrews 8:10.

A SHOW YOUR MONEY WHO'S BOSS EXERCISE

An easy way to begin to gain control of your spending is this. The next time you plan to go to the grocery store on your way home from work make a shopping list. That is easy enough. Now comes the hard part. Decide in advance and write down how much you will spend. At some point during the day stop by the bank or an ATM and withdraw that exact amount of cash and no more. Go buy your groceries and keep the total tab at or under your predetermined amount. "That is easy enough; if I run over I can always use my debit card." No you can't...here is the hardest part. Leave your credit cards at home, and leave your debit card in your car so that it is unavailable to you while you are inside the store. This will offer good training for you to begin gaining control of and limiting your spending. Try it a few times. When you have learned to make it work for one store, add a second store. Perhaps a clothing store, a shoe store, or a sporting goods store.

If this method doesn't work so well for you the first time you try it, don't be discouraged. Hardly anyone feels comfortable shopping like this at first. Try it again, it really does work. You need to give it an ample opportunity to work for you. After you have tried it a few times, it will become very natural and you will love the new sense of freedom and empowerment it gives you. If you are still having trouble after several attempts, then ask someone to go shopping with you to serve as an encourager and as your accountability partner. If TV shopping channels or the Internet are the problem you may need to make some extreme choices. Either block them from your list of available channels or have the cable company unhook their service from your home. You may also have to remove access to the Internet on your computer as well. "And the peace of God, which transcends all understanding, will guard your hearts and your minds in Christ Jesus" Philippians 4:7.

3. Hyperactive Spending

This type of spending is totally out of control. Chances are that you know someone who has gone on a hyper spending spree at some point in their life. Remember the guy and the free cooler? That certainly was impulsive, but it was also hyper. Any unplanned big-ticket item, like a $25,000 purchase is an example of hyper spending. Now, before you get upset…look at the key word of that last sentence…UNPLANNED. Buying a new car, or a new house, or a new diamond ring is neither necessarily hyper nor impulsive. The key concept is that the purchase was UNPLANNED. When you are in control of your spending you are just that…in control. You plan your purchases and make them when you can afford them. That concept is so simple, yet so profound. What a novel concept. The very idea of actually planning to buy a new car or a new diamond ring is foreign to some people. No, it's not a novel concept. It shows maturity, self-discipline, and self-control over spending. These are good things.

Some Hyper Spending has a Medical Origin

If you have symptoms of hyper spending that you think may be linked to a medical condition (Bipolar disorder,) please do yourself and your family a favor and see your medical doctor for his advice and possible treatment.

Helpful Principles for Dealing with Financial ADHD

Retrain Your Thinking

You take charge of your thinking. Ask God to enable you to begin to see money and financial matters differently. Partner with someone who has good spending habits and ask them to mentor you in spending and finances. Ask them to go shopping with you and act as a spending coach. The key here will be to partner with someone who is good at managing their money and thinks correctly about money and spending. "Therefore, prepare your minds for action; be self-controlled; set your hope fully on the grace to be given you when Jesus Christ is revealed" I Peter 1:13. "You will keep in perfect peace him whose mind is steadfast, because he trusts in you" Isaiah 26:3.

SEE MONEY FOR WHAT IT REALLY IS

Money is no more than a medium of exchange. Before paper and plastic money were invented, people used other things for currency: beads, animal pelts, precious stones, silver nuggets, gold dust, in exchange for food and other necessities. Learn to view money for what it really is. It is just paper or plastic. You trade a handful of paper bills for a few sacks of groceries, for a tank of gas, for a place to live, and for a cool or warm house or apartment. Get it? Money is nothing more than pieces of paper that you exchange for goods or services.

Learn to keep money in a proper perspective. Money is important because it enables us to enjoy some of the basic needs and wants of life. It would be hard to make a house, car, or utility payment with only a handshake and a smile. Unfortunately, buying groceries or clothes takes a little more than a nod, a pat on the back, and a few kind words of thanks. Money is a necessary medium of exchange in all cultures. Sure, we all would probably like to have a little more of it from time to time, but money isn't everything. God has an insightful word of truth to enable us to view money in the proper perspective. "For the love of money is a root of all kinds of evil. Some people, eager for money, have wandered from the faith and pierced themselves with many griefs" I Timothy 6:10. Two things to note are what God said, and what he didn't say. First, he didn't say that money is the root of evil. He did say that the LOVE of money is the root of all kinds of evil. He said that eagerness for money has caused some to wander from the faith and that they have pierced themselves with many griefs. Money is important, but how many people do you know that would be better off today had they not had so much money to manage? Money is not sinful. Wealth and riches are not sinful. The sin comes when people have ungodly attitudes, actions, and love for money. Jesus NEVER condemned rich people for their riches. Jesus NEVER condemned poor people for their poverty. Thank God for rich people who have a godly perspective toward money. God uses them and their money to accomplish great things in his Kingdom. Thank God for poor people who have a godly perspective toward money. God uses them and their lack of money to accomplish great things in his Kingdom. No matter where you lie along the scale of riches or poverty, the Lord loves you and wants to use your life and your resources for his glory. Check out the perspective of the following rich man.

A very wealthy man died and his relatives honored his last wish. He wanted to be buried in a coffin filled with sacks containing his gold coin collection that was worth $100,000. He arrived in Heaven carrying all his gold coins and was greeted by St. Peter. Peter had a puzzled look on his face when he welcomed him to Heaven: "Hi, James, I'm Peter, welcome to God's Kingdom. I will show you your mansion in a minute, but you have piqued my curiosity and I just have to ask one question before we go any farther." James said: "Thanks, go ahead and ask." Diplomatically, Peter responded: "James, I'm just wondering, what on earth possessed you to bring those sacks of gold with you to Heaven?" James responded: "Why, Peter, its gold and it's worth a fortune." Peter replied: "James you brought sacks of pavement with you to Heaven. Pavement, it's just pavement, don't you see that all our streets here are paved with gold." People in Heaven are walking on gold right now. That takes some of the luster away doesn't it? Paper money, plastic debit cards, gold, silver, and coins of all types are just a medium of exchange.

Compared to other important things such as relationships with your family and friends and service to God, money is nothing more than pavement. Yet money can get us into trouble lots of times because we place far too much importance upon it. "Your attitude should be the same as that of Christ Jesus" Philippians 2:5.

DON'T FEAR MONEY OR SPENDING

There is no reason to be afraid of spending money. You have to spend money for your necessities and some of your wants of life. It is perfectly natural to need and want some of the finer things in life. Bring balance into your life by balancing your needs and wants. It is sinful to want some nice things? Not necessarily, it is great to want to enjoy and to give nice things to those you love. Balance is being able to discern between what we need and want and how much we can afford. In Philippians 4:19 the Lord promised to supply all our needs by his riches in glory. By needs, he is talking about the basic necessities of life that we have to have in order to live. God will also grant some of our wants as well. He will not give us all our wants, only the ones he knows would benefit us. "For God did not give us a spirit of timidity, but a spirit of power, of love, and of self-discipline" 2 Timothy 1:7.

CHALLENGE YOUR THINKING

LONG TERM THINKING

Long term thinking is best illustrated by the Chinese proverb. "Give a man a fish and you feed him for a day. Teach a man to fish and you feed him for a lifetime."

Every homeowner has captured a piece of long term thinking. If you sign up to make 360 payments on a house over a span of 30 years, you are engaged in long term thinking. Either deliberately or inadvertently, you are planning 30 years into your future. If you are a home buyer and are age 25 and add the 30 years of your home loan to your age, you get 55. Wow. You are actually planning something that will happen when you are 55 years old. If you are 25 and contributing to an IRA retirement account at work you are planning some 40 years out into your future. You may have never thought of it like that before. You may be involved in long term, or forward thinking, either deliberately or unintentionally. At any rate, you are doing some long term thinking and planning. Regardless of your age, if you are a Christian who has accepted Jesus as your Lord and Savior you are planning millions of years into your future…it's called Heaven.

Long term thinking is linear…like a long line. Long term thinking concerns anything that is five or more years out from today. It could be your graduation. It could be your future marriage, future children, future career change, or future retirement. It is anything that is five or more years ahead in your future.

Long term thinking relates to your finances as you plan for your financial future. It could involve a long awaited vacation, saving up cash for your new car, funding your emergency fund, stashing away money for a child's college education, saving to buy your own house, setting aside money for your retirement, or anything five or more years ahead in your future. As you plan and save and plan and spend you are sowing seeds for a more prosperous future. You are engaged in forward thinking, not just here and now thinking. Prepare for the future. Keep up your good work. You will really be happy you did one day.

Short term thinking

Sadly, too many people are affected by a degree of short term thinking. Short term thinkers live for today and perhaps even for the rest of the week, but that's about it. They can hardly see beyond their noses. They adopt the old Epicurean motto of: "Eat, drink, and be merry, for tomorrow we die." These people have neither concern for nor plan for tomorrow. They are well represented within the group of people who live paycheck to paycheck. A definitive study hasn't been done to determine just how many people are living paycheck to paycheck, but estimates range from 30%-50% of Americans live under that curse. One thing is for sure; however, more than 50% of Americans are only two or three missed paychecks away from financial ruin.

Learn How to Fish

One of the major purposes of this book it that of attempting to teach people how to fish, Jesus taught his disciples how to fish in Luke 5:1-11, and John 21:1-14. And, oh did they ever become experts. Unfortunately, many within our society have bought into the "Give a man a fish and you feed him for a day…" mentality. One of the greatest civil injustices in the history of the United States is the fact that many social and government programs have done nothing but create a dependent class of people sometimes called the "underclass." These are people who have been robbed of their dignity, hope, and self-respect. They have been conned out of the desire to work and make something out of themselves. Many seem to have lost the motivation to live. Unfortunately, some have almost lost their very souls.

The Lord wants you to learn how to fish. In John 6:1-15, Jesus was faced by thousands of hungry people who needed food. He performed a miracle and fed the crowd of people all the food they wanted. They were amazed at his miraculous powers and were extremely thankful for the food. In their exuberance, they wanted to stay in Jesus' presence, make him King, and allow him to provide their daily needs. Jesus refused to be a "Bread Messiah," so he sent them back to their homes. The Scriptures give us the idea that he wanted them to learn how to fish and not merely be given a fish to eat each day. The Lord wishes to enable you to benefit from the common sense principles of financial freedom taught by the Bible. God is Awesome and he wants to teach you to fish, not merely give you a fish each day. Are you learning?

IT'S YOUR MONEY

You have a lot of options when it comes to managing your money. You can spend it, save it, invest it, spend it wisely, or pile it up in the back yard and have a bonfire with it. It all comes back to you and your decisions. Decide now that you are going to work to achieve a sense of balance in your life when it comes to money. You can learn to control your money and not allow it to control you. As you make strides in this area you will begin to experience financial freedom that you once only imagined.

"Therefore, prepare your minds for action; be self-controlled; set your hope fully on the grace to be given you when Jesus Christ is revealed" I Peter 1:13.

Chapter 9
Taming the Financial Crises Monsters

Since you are reading this book you may be engaged in a battle to survive your own personal financial crisis. Your goal is survival for you and your family. But wouldn't it be great to do more than just survive. What if you could emerge from this experience in an even better financial situation than you were in when your personal financial crisis developed? What if you became a stronger person and a stronger family as well? What if you not only survived your crisis, but learned principles and truths to enable you to excel in survival mode?

ETERNAL TRUTH: WHILE GOD DOES NOT ALWAYS REMOVE YOUR PROBLEMS, HE IS WILLING, READY, AND ABLE TO GUIDE AND EQUIP YOU IN WORKING THROUGH THEM.

Some just graduated college and are starting a career. It is imperative that you survive the financial storms that will come your way. You have your whole life in front of you. Others are in the process of starting over, and wish to lessen the risk of losing all the ground you have gained. Still others know that survival is your only option because you have dependent children and your family's very survival depends upon you.

You are feeling the pressure. Take heart, you are going to make it. Survival means different things to different people. To some it means keeping your current job, to others it means earning a promotion, becoming a supervisor, landing a better job, changing careers, going into business for oneself, or leading their business to survive. Wherever you are in the spectrum, you want to be able to look back one day and say that you succeeded in spite of the worst economy since 1929.

I have designed a plan to assist people in taming the money monster of financial storms, and of achieving some of their financial goals. The following story helps illustrate many of its principles. Envision yourself in this scenario.

You are a Captain in the United States Marine Corps and are flying a mission over hostile territory. You are alone in the cockpit of your fighter when it is hit by a surface-to-air missile; quickly you evaluate your situation and make the split-second decision to eject from your fatally stricken aircraft.

Your only thought is survival. Instinctively you rely upon all your training and go into SURVIVAL MODE as you punch out and "hit the silk." As your chute opens you pray the most sincere prayer you have prayed in a while. Your earthward journey seems to last forever. Fearing that a sniper may pick you off in mid-air, you are relieved when you realize that the ground is rushing to meet you at a welcoming speed. As you prepare to land you begin rehearsing your next moves. You don't even have to think about what to do because your survival training kicks in. As soon as your feet touch the ground, you spring into action, you…

GET TOUGH: you are afraid, your heart is racing, you lock into the right frame of mind, mentally and emotionally you prepare to survive, you shift into survival mode, you just landed in enemy territory.

ASSESS THE SITUATION: you check for wounds, injuries, and reach for your survival kit.

RE-ORIENT YOURSELF: you are no longer in your aircraft, you are in enemy territory, and they will capture you, possibly torture you, or even kill you, you must determine where you are and where you need to go from here.

STREAMLINE: you cast off all unnecessary items, parachute, harnesses, flight helmet and leave them behind.

CONSERVE RESOURCES: you conserve what you have left, food water, survival manual, weapon, survival tools.

Seek New Resources: you add water, food, and necessities to what you already have.

Seek Shelter: a place to get out of the elements, and escape the harsh environment.

Seek Safety: a place to hide, a place where you will rest, recuperate, recharge, plan, and await rescue.

Develop a Plan of Attack: you plan to survive, to get out alive. You know that your family and all of your shipmates will be praying for you and anxiously awaiting your rescue. You also know that your training, your attitude, this experience itself, and your faith in God will make you a better person if you can just survive.

Assess Strength of Enemy: Who are they? How many are there? Where are they? What direction will the possible attacks come from?

Prepare to Fight to Survive: you target the enemy only if necessary, the best fight is the one you are able to avoid completely.

Move to Safety: you move to higher ground, out of harm's way.

Contact Rescuers: you radio for a rescue pickup.

Maintain your Lifelines: you rely upon God. You have the assurance that he will allow you to be reunited with your family, friends, fellow Marines, and your church family one day soon. You look forward to being debriefed and rejoining your unit, for you will have survived the most harrowing ordeal of your life.

Develop your Personal Plan of Action

One of the greatest principles in all the universe is found in the New Testament book of Romans 8:23. "And we know that in all things God works for the good of those who love him, who have been called according to his purpose."

Eternal Truth: God works for good in all things for those who love him and are called according to his purpose.

Imagine that…Jesus is able to take the most horrific experience of your entire life and bring something good from it. God works in all things, not just the good things of life. This actually means that the Lord is able to take the most evil circumstance you have ever experienced and bring something good out of it. Jesus offers this wonderful promise to those who love him and who have personally accepted him as their Lord and Savior. Bad things do happen to good people. Evil is present in the world and satanic forces motivate ungodly people to commit all manner of vile and sinful acts. Almost every person alive has been on the receiving end of someone else's sinful behavior. Even though God never causes sinful acts, events, behaviors, or outcomes to happen, he can work through the most wicked of all circumstances to bring something good out of them and into your life. This verse does not say that God is working to see that we are always happy or that our lives are filled with only good things. It does say that the Lord is working within our lives for his own glory and is bringing good things out of evil things in order to accomplish his purposes within Christians' lives. Allow this verse to give you a new perspective on life. If you love Jesus and desire to serve him, he is constantly working to bring good things into your life.

God is always present, even within your personal crises. He is always there to bring something good from each and every situation you will ever experience. In the center of a personal financial crisis, learn to trust in God and not your personal possessions and treasures. Your greatest security is in Heaven, not your bank, your career, and your earthly possessions. Evil things happen to you and me because we are sinful and we live in a world filled with sinful people who commit sinful acts. With the Lord's help we can learn to accept the fact that parts of our lives will be very rough, even painful. As we mature in our Christian walks we learn to begin looking for and then finding the good that God is able to bring out of our worst experiences.

The following fourteen principles will equip you to survive most of the personal crises of life. They are valid principles of survival and will work for anyone. However, Christians have an edge on surviving, because the Lord is actively working within his or her life to bring them through anything they may experience.

Principles of Survival

1. Get Tough

You have landed right in the center of your own personal financial crisis. You feel helpless and out of control. You feel as though your money is controlling you and that you have no control over your finances. You feel as though you have been blindsided because you didn't ask for this and you didn't know it was coming. But now it's here. Gripped with fear, or in some cases, pure terror, your heart is racing, you sometimes feel depressed, as though your world has caved in upon you. For some it has. It may be a home mortgage gone bust. It could be the loss of your job, your spouses' job, bankruptcy, the failure of your business, the demise of your 401(k), the death of a family member, a repossessed automobile, or a myriad of other problems. You feel like it is time to quit. You have reached the point where despair has taken over and hopelessness has kicked in. You don't know what to do, where to go, or what is going to happen to you.

Instead of quitting, you decide that it is time to get tough. It is time for action. It is time to develop a plan and fight for your and your family's financial, emotional, and spiritual survival. In a crisis many people turn to everyone for help except the one who can help them the most. They turn to the government, their bank, their employer, their best friend, self-help books, their accountant, their attorney, and so on. When really significant crises come the very best place one can turn is to turn to the Lord. "God is our refuge and strength, an ever-present help in trouble" Psalm 46:1. Yes, it is time for action. But it is time for the right kind of action. Some things will help you right now while other things will not.

Imagine that you are walking beside a swimming pool, you can't swim, and you accidentally trip and fall into 10 feet of water. What do you need: a fire extinguisher, a can of soda, your favorite CD, your Ipod? No, you need a life preserver. When people fall into the seas of personal crises they often grab for the wrong things. They grab for things that would be good in many other circumstances but that will not help at all when they are drowning.

Now is the time to get tough. Now is the time to look for a job, create a job, change careers, or find housing. Now is the time to salvage what you can out of your crisis. How does one get tough? The very best way to get tough is to follow the advice of the Lord given in his Word. "Therefore, prepare your minds for action; be self-controlled; set your hope fully on the grace to be given to you when Jesus Christ is revealed" 1 Peter 1:13. Now is the time for financial and spiritual warfare. Now is the time for prayer, and personal Bible study. Now is the time to become involved in a truly Bible-believing church that will offer emotional and spiritual support, and a place for service for you and your family.

2. Assess your Situation

This is the time for assessment and evaluation of your personal financial situation. At this point, you check for wounds, injuries, survey the damage, and reach for your survival kit. "What survival kit?" you say. Don't worry; by the time you finish this book you will know how to prepare a financial survival strategy for yourself and your family that will be there for the next crisis you face.

Assessment involves examining one's total situation. Now is the time to be 100% honest concerning your bank accounts, your monthly expenditures, your income, your job security or job insecurity, your 401(k)s, and everything else you can think of. Put it on a spreadsheet or a piece of paper and get it all out in the open in order to get a clear view of the overall situation. Avoid blame at all costs. If your spouse just lost his or her job, the last thing they need to hear is something like: "I tried to tell you to look for another job last year." If your spouse amassed a huge credit card debt and it is overwhelming the budget, there are ways to resolve the issue. If you defaulted on your mortgage and are having to live with a relative, there is no need to blame one another for the situation. It is time to come together and work as a team and work through the situation.

For survival to be a possibility you will have to confront reality at this time. Now is not the time to gloss over your financial problems or pitfalls. For example: if you have a gallbladder attack, and your doctor recommends immediate emergency surgery, the last thing you need to do is to ignore the problem. You would need to act and act immediately or face unwelcomed consequences. You may choose to ignore your financial problems. With almost 100% certainty, you know that your situation will only get worse if you wait. Now is the time to assess and evaluate where you are and then develop a plan of attack.

One of the anchor points in your survival kit will be the Bible. The Lord has a word for this situation in 2 Timothy 2:15: "Do your best to present yourself to God as one approved, a workman who does not need to be ashamed and who correctly handles the word of truth." Yes, this verse is referring to discipleship and studying the Word of God. Studying the word of God for answers to life's problems is one of the practical benefits of the Christian life. God has answers to each and every problem or for every conceivable situation in which one could ever find himself. He has solutions for your financial distress. You will discover many as you read on.

3. REORIENT YOURSELF TOWARD JESUS

No matter where you are right now, or no matter where you have been, there is hope for your future. You can both learn and practice sound financial principles. Your can enter on a course of action that will virtually guarantee that your life will be totally different one year from today. Now is the time to get a new course heading for the rest of your life.

Your financial crisis may be crying out for a true transformation. A transformation takes place when things are changed from what they are now and become something totally different. A transformation is a metamorphosis. Do you remember studying the fact that a caterpillar crawls up a twig, spins a silken cocoon around itself, and then emerges as a beautiful butterfly after the metamorphosis takes place? You can experience your own personal transformation or metamorphosis. An example would be that of being in total financial chaos and moving from that state of confusion to a state of total financial order and peace.

No one said it would be easy or painless. Quite the contrary; change may hurt, and it may hurt a lot. You will have to decide how much change you want, need, and how badly you want it. The athletes who perform in the Olympics have spent thousands of hours in training.

The same is true of the concert pianist. If you want to succeed beyond what the average person will experience, you may have to make some tough choices that could bring major changes to your situation. Positive change is possible. Just as night is transformed into day and winter is transformed into summer, God can transform your life by transforming your attitude and outlook. He can transform the way you respond to crisis situations and material things. He can also change the way you think and respond to him. If you truly put Christ first in your life, everything else will begin to become reoriented and become reprioritized. Matthew 6:33 says: "But seek first his kingdom and his righteousness, and all these things will be given to you as well."

Depending upon the severity of your financial situation, order may come almost instantly. For others it may take a week or two. Still others may require a few months or years. If you have spent the past ten years living carelessly and getting yourself into a nightmarish financial situation wrought with debt and an almost insurmountable mountain to climb, it will take some time to get out. Don't expect God to simply drop a $1,000,000 dollar cashier's check into your lap. Even if he did, some would go on a spending binge. After the smoke cleared, their bills would have doubled.

Do expect God to help you follow his will and devise a plan. Next, work that plan to get your life back in order. With his help and with much prayer and Bible study determine where you are. Review how you got there. Determine where you need to go. Develop a godly plan of action to help you get to where you need to be. Romans 12:2: "Do not conform any longer to the pattern of this world, but be transformed by the renewing of your mind. Then you will be able to test and approve what God's will is—his good, pleasing and perfect will." You can succeed through the Lord's help.

4. STREAMLINE

Can you imagine a world record holding Olympic sprinter approaching the starting blocks to run his or her favorite race while wearing a 60 pound backpack? The crowd and all the other sprinters would focus their full attention upon that runner. They would be wondering whether the runner was crazy since no one has ever attempted to run an Olympic race while wearing a backpack. The racers take their stances, the official fires the starting gun, the backpack is still in place. The record holding sprinter is guaranteed not to win the race and, in fact, finishes dead last. This is an almost impossible scenario. However, it does illustrate the point that there may be some things in your life that you need to lay aside. You may already know what they are because you have thought about them before. They are the very things that are impeding your success at home and on the job. You know, some of the things that are holding you and your family back financially, relationally, attitudinally, developmentally, and spiritually.

Are you carrying a 60 pound backpack through life? If you are, now is the time for you to lay aside all that you may have been carrying on your back for a while. Your backpack may be filled with one or more of the following sins, destructive or addictive behaviors, harmful habits, or lifestyle choices like guilt, shame, blame, bad attitude, idolatry (worship of things, people, or anything that comes before God) an unforgiving spirit, faultfinding, anger, rage, bad spending habits, or debt. Other baggage might include pride, lust, greed, gluttony, trust in money, overspending, stealing, gambling, alcoholism, smoking, drugs, pornography, adultery, pre-marital sex, abortion, homosexuality, religion, or anything else that keeps you from enjoying the freedom, forgiveness, love, and acceptance that God wishes for you to experience and enjoy.

ETERNAL TRUTH: No matter what you have been carrying around in your personal life, God loves you unconditionally. There is nothing you have done that God can't forgive. No sin or sins are bigger than God's power to forgive. No matter where you are right now nor where you have been in your past, God is willing to forgive you and give you a fresh start.

Remember that Jesus loves you with an irrevocable, eternal love. You can't lose his love. It is unconditional, and is based on his unchanging integrity and character—-not on your behavior. That does not mean that he condones sin. All sin and ungodly behavior is destructive; therefore, God despises it. The Lord wants you to be set free from the things that are destructive to you and to others in your life. By consciously turning away from them and turning to Jesus, their power over you can be broken and replaced by the freedom and enjoyment God wants for your life. The Lord's affection and unfailing love for you is not based on what you do. You can't earn it or work to keep it. When you fail, you do not forfeit his love. There is nothing you can do to persuade God not to love you. His love and forgiveness is freely given, and all you have to do is open your heart and receive it.

Agree with God that you, just like everyone else in the world, are a sinner. Turn away from your sins, destructive or addictive behaviors, habits, or lifestyles, and ask the Lord to adopt you as a full member of his family. He will come into your life. He never has turned anyone down who has asked him for his gift of grace and a relationship with him.

One of the most surprising things that can keep one away from God is religion. Religion is man-made. Man sometimes corrupts true faith by either adding extra things to it, or by removing or diluting some of the teachings of the Bible in order to make it more acceptable or palatable to their own needs. Many have exchanged religion for a true relationship with Christ. Begin your own personal relationship with Christ today. Avoid the counterfeit…religion.

These are some of the many things that always hold people back. Why load your life down with excess baggage? Travel light. Do yourself a favor and cast off all unnecessary encumbrances. Discard anything and everything that could hold you back or impede your progress toward your goal of coming out of this crisis successfully. It is time to jettison the 60 pound backpack and win your race. "Therefore…let us throw off everything that hinders and the sin that so easily entangles, and let us run with perseverance the race marked out for us" Hebrews 12:1.

5. Conserve your Resources

To be realistic and painfully honest, some may never get back to the place you once were financially. Others will not only get back to where they were; they will get there and then go far beyond that level of living. But remember, all of that stuff was just that…stuff.

You once got along without it, and you can survive if you have to get along without it once again. Remember a man named Job and the misery he endured? He gave some poignant advice when he said: "Naked I came from my mother's womb, and naked I will depart. The Lord gave and the Lord has taken away; may the name of the Lord be praised" Job 1:21.

Job had the proper perspective. At one time in his life he had everything he ever wanted. But, he went from having everything to that of having absolutely nothing left but his own life, God, his wife, and three friends. The most important things you can preserve are your relationship with God, yourself, and your family. Believe it or not, one can replace a house, a job, a career, a car, and so forth. While it may seem totally impossible to you at the moment, those things are replaceable.

Admittedly, you may have taken a big hit. Ask God to give you the kind of perspective we read about in Job's life. He came into the world with nothing, he took nothing with him when he died, and he confidently blessed the name of the Lord. "Give thanks in all circumstances," are some of the best words of advice one can relate to in the during trying times. Paul gives these words in I Thessalonians 5:16-18: "Rejoice always, pray continually, give thanks in all circumstances; for this is God's will for you in Christ Jesus." Admittedly, these three commands are very tough for some people to wrap their minds around and put into practice during times of crisis. Even though they are radical, they are true, and can change your life entirely.

If one is not a Christian, these commands make absolutely no sense at all. Why? Because it is only through Christ's strength that anyone can put them into practice in the while in the throes of a crisis. Ask God for help. Concentrate upon your own life and family. Do everything within your power to preserve them. Pray for God's help and wisdom to heal the wounds and hurts in your family relationships. After discarding all unnecessary encumbrances, keep what you have left. Conserve your resources and avoid any and all frivolous expenditures. The Bible is a key point in your survival manual. Heed its truths and spend your resources very wisely. "Discretion will protect you, and understanding will guard you…" Proverbs 2:11, and, "You are my hiding place; you will protect me from trouble and surround me with songs of deliverance" Psalm 32:7.

6. Seek New Resources

Surviving the crises in your life may rely upon how well you are able to appropriate new resources. The average person has more resources available to him than he might realize.

Call upon your network of church, family, friends, neighbors, and fellow employees and begin to gather the resources you need. A few may be in such terrible financial desperation that they will have to find help by calling upon a church, a local food bank, the Salvation Army, the Department of Health and Human Services, or a local homeless shelter. Should you have all that you need, consider donating some of your extra food, clothing, or money to a needy family or to one of the organizations mentioned above.

Seek the strongest resource of all, the Lord and his wonderful Word. Study and memorize your favorite verses from his Word. "I have hidden your word in my heart that I might not sin against you" Psalm 119:11. Seek God's wisdom through prayer and Bible study and let him guide you as you plan to get out of the current crisis. Seek food, both spiritual food and physical food. Seek God's wisdom and direction, use this time in your life to learn to keep your eyes focused upon him.

7. Seek Shelter

Daniel spent the night in one of the most inhospitable places on earth, the Lion's den. His enemies had him thrown into the den of lions for breaking a law that had been enacted specifically to keep him from praying and worshipping the Lord. Daniel's detractors hated him and were attempting to have him killed, but their malicious plan backfired. God was there with Daniel, and the Scriptures tell us that God simply shut the mouths of the lions (Daniel 6:22).

In a crisis, you and your family need shelter. First, seek the spiritual shelter of the very presence of the Lord. He can shelter and protect you. Next, seek physical shelter. Keep your house if you possibly can. Ask others for help. If you have to leave, leave as gracefully as you possibly can and in a way that honors God. Muster all the faith you have and ask God to provide for you. Go to him in prayer and pour your heart out to him.

Ask for guidance and wisdom. Ask him to lead you as you seek help from family, friends, your church, or the benevolent organizations already mentioned above. Ask God to move you to the safest and the best place on earth you can possibly be...the very center of his will.

Eternal truth: God may have you down in the trenches in order to teach you some things he wants you to learn that you would have never learned anywhere else.

Some of the greatest and deepest lessons learned by many Christians came only after they reached some of the lowest points in their lives. One such believer who knew what trouble was all about was a man named David. Learn from his words: "Have mercy on me, O God, have mercy on me, for in you my soul takes refuge. I will take refuge in the shadow of your wings until the disaster has passed" Psalm 57:1.

8. Seek Safety

Some people have safe rooms built into their houses. Others have storm shelters. A few have even built up a small arsenal of weapons to protect their lives and property. Still others seek the safety of a Swiss Bank Account. Safety is important. Ask any airline passenger. Ask those who work around jet aircraft with running engines. Ask firefighters, rescue personnel, soldiers, industrial workers, railroaders, and countless others that spend a good portion of their careers studying, training, and in reviewing safety procedures and practices.

Seek safety as you deal with your financial crisis. Avoid additional debts or any circumstances that would make a terrible situation worse: unemployment, a housing foreclosure, or bankruptcy. Most importantly, seek the safety and security of the Lord. Only he can give you the true peace and safety that you need. Job said: "You will be secure, because there is hope; you will look about you and take your rest in safety" Job 11:18. King David said: "I will lie down and sleep in peace, for you alone, O Lord, make me dwell in safety" Psalm 4:8.

9. Develop Your Plan of Attack

A boy received his first bow and arrows for Christmas when he was 13 years old. After target practicing all day, he realized that he was not able to hit the target very often. He came up with a brilliant strategy. He shot six arrows into the side of the family garage, took some black paint and painted concentric circles around each one of them. He then brought all his friends over to his house, showed them the six arrows centered in each of the targets, and bragged about what a good shot he was. His results looked great. But his aim was lousy.

In order to survive and succeed in your financial crisis you will need a plan. Unless you are either rich or crazy, you can't afford to shoot all your arrows and then draw your targets around them. You will first need to identify the targets you wish to hit, and then, and only then, step back and shoot your arrows. No one can do this for you; you have to decide upon the best targets for you and your family. If you don't have a target at which to aim, all your shots at success will randomly fly off into the air and will not accomplish anything of lasting value.

As you begin, ask for and seek the Lord's wisdom and guidance. Seek his will as you develop your plan. Again, no one can do this for you; you have to develop this for yourself. If you attempt to have someone else decide your targets for you, they will not be your targets. They would only be their best guesses of what you need to do to get back upon a firm footing. However, others can assist you in identifying your targets or formulating your plans to hit them. There are many Christian resources, other Christians, and a host of other helps that are available: your pastor, CPA, broker, attorney, HR person, best friend, brother-in-law, family member, this and other Christian books, and the list goes on.

Take action and decide who you need to consult for advice and direction. Sit down and prayerfully make a list of your best resources. Discuss this list with your spouse or family. Come to an agreement, develop a plan of attack, and then write it down. By this time you have done most of the hard work. Now that you have a plan, the next phase is to implement it.

One of the greatest mistakes many Christians make is that they work arduously to map out their plans. They struggle with them, discuss them, and have others critique them. They write them down, revise them, and write them down again another time or two. Finally, they have a plan that they feel would be good enough to solve the financial problems of millions of people. They are so proud of themselves. Endless hours have been spent developing their plan. It is wonderful, it is revolutionary. It will bring unbridled success. In their excitement they bow their heads and thank the Lord for the plan they designed and then they ask him to do one simple thing. They pray: "Lord, please bless my plan." There is a major problem with this approach. What is the problem? Right, you have already figured it out. Rather than go to the Lord and ask him to bless something after the fact: "Lord, bless this mess." One is much more likely to succeed when involving the Lord at every step of the planning process. In fact, when the Lord is truly involved in your planning process, your plan is guaranteed to work so long as you follow it precisely to the nth degree. God had these words of wisdom for us in James 4:13-17: "Now listen, you who say, 'Today or tomorrow we will go to this or that city, spend a year there, carry on business and make money.' Why, you do not even know what will happen tomorrow. What is your life? You are a mist that appears for a little while and then vanishes. Instead, you ought to say, 'If it is the Lord's will, we will live and do this or that.' As it is, you boast and brag. All such boasting is evil. Anyone, then, who knows the good he ought to do and doesn't do it, sins."

As a Christian undergoing a crisis situation your major objectives include: to survive and get out of your crisis alive; to discover the good things God is bringing out of a bad situation; to find God's will for your life; to emerge stronger than when you entered your crisis; and to learn, grow, and mature as a result of going through your personal crisis. Without the aim of the Master's hand your plans won't achieve a lot of lasting results.

10. Assess the Strength of Your Enemy The first assessment you need to make is spiritual in nature. Satan will attack you in many ways and in the middle of many of life's circumstances, tragedies, and crises. "Be self-controlled and alert. Your enemy the devil prowls around like a roaring lion looking for someone to devour" 1 Peter 5:8. Know who you are facing in battle. Remember, the human mind is the battleground where Satan launches his attacks. All temptations are introduced through your mind and its thought processes. Anticipate that his attacks will come from all directions and from unusual places. Satan will attack your weaknesses and your strengths. He will attack you in the same ways he has attacked you before. He will attack you in new and unusual ways as well. He will even use family members, friends, coworkers, and total strangers.

Don't underestimate his power. Satan is a formidable foe. But in reality, when compared to God's power, his power is like that of a birthday candle compared to the power of the sun. If you are a true child of the God and are earnestly trying to live within the Lord's will for your life, Satan has virtually no power over you at all. If you are not a Christian, you have no power over him at all.

If you are a born again Christian, he can't make you do anything. Sure, he will tempt you but he can't possibly force you to sin. God won't let him. He will attack you with every type of temptation you can possibly imagine and in ways you have never even considered. He is crafty. But as a true child of God, you have the right to stand firm within the power of Christ. Learn to say the words Jesus said to him: "Get thee behind me, Satan" Matthew 4:10.

You have to know who you are fighting and understand his tactics before you can expect to win the fight. In addition to any other issues you are struggling with, you are battling an economy that has gone south. You may be the victim of a layoff, a sub-prime mortgage, a bankruptcy, the careless use of credit cards or car loans, or the stock market that dropped precipitously and lost more than a trillion dollars. Many people are living in the aftermath of bad decisions they made in the past that are now rearing their ugly heads in revenge. Look at your personal situation and identify which things are attacking your financial integrity. Once you identify those things you will know who to fight and then you can develop the plan you need to make your fight successful.

11. Prepare to Fight for Your Survival

When in survival mode you may have to fight for your life. However, you will need to choose your battles carefully. Depending upon your individual circumstances, you may have to engage in a life or death struggle as you battle for your financial life. If you fall behind on your mortgage payments the first thing to do is to pray and ask the Lord for guidance and then make an appointment with your mortgage company to work out arrangements to satisfy your debt. Believe it or not, they really do not want to foreclose on your house. They would much rather you keep it and make payments. They know that if they have to foreclose and then either have to list it with a realtor or auction it off, they may lose tens of thousands of dollars. Go talk to them. Work out a payment schedule that will allow you to stay in your house and make a minimum payment to the bank for a predetermined period of time. Who knows, they may even work with you to refinance your loan at a better rate than you had before, that would lower your monthly payment. The same strategy may also work with your auto loan, your home equity loan, and some of your consumer credit card loans. Take the first step. Don't wait until you receive the dreaded letter from your lender, bank, mortgage company, or credit card company. Take action; get out in front of their plan to contact you wanting their money.

Credit card debt is another area where you may need to battle for your financial life. If you are unemployed, or are so deeply in debt that you are having a tough time making payments, you can call your credit card company and ask them to lower your interest rate. If you have been late with some of your payments or have had other problems with your creditors, don't expect miracles. But it never hurts to ask. A word of caution…late payments, or charging over the card's limit usually results in a credit card company raising interest rates to more than 30% APR. Don't be late…even by one day.

TV and radio commercials highlight the next possible option to battle this situation…consolidate your credit card debts into one debt. This is a very risky move, however, because many of the so called "Debt Settlement Companies," are nothing but fronts for consumer scams. These scams have become so widespread that many states' attorneys general have begun prosecuting these companies and putting them out of business. Consolidating debts is also a risky move, because many consumers who have exercised the debt consolidation option make one gargantuan mistake. They resume their old spending and charging practices and run the balances on the cards they just zeroed out back up to the max. The only thing this accomplishes is that their debts virtually double. It is not uncommon for a person to see their debt level rise from $10,000 to $20,000 within a year or less. Plus, they will have paid a debt consolidation company a hefty fee for their services, not to mention the negative mark such a move places on your credit report…it appears like a bankruptcy. You are advised not to use this option. If you choose to pursue this tactic, be sure and educate yourself first and examine all the ramifications of this decision. Before you do anything, seek godly wisdom and financial council. A much better plan is that of starting with the card that has the smallest balance and pay it off completely. Next, choose the card with the next highest balance and pay it off. Then choose the third card and the fourth card and follow the same plan. This approach will be outlined in much greater detail in Chapter 11, *Taming the Debt Monster*.

So far we have been talking about some of the financial and economic battles of life. Now let's take a look at how these battles are also spiritual in nature and how the Lord can enable you to have victory in them.

The fact is that Satan will attempt to insert his influence into any battle we allow him to get involved with in our lives. He can take aim at you through your job or jobless situation, your house payment or foreclosure, your exorbitant credit card debts or the money you have saved or invested, your health, your family, or anything else you allow him to have influence upon. Virtually any area of your life can come under satanic attack.

Here is a guaranteed formula for success in your spiritual fight against the enemy. Rather than fight the enemy yourself, ask the Lord fight him for you. "For the Lord your God is the one who goes with you to fight for you against your enemies to give you victory" Deuteronomy 20:4. Another verse that supports this idea of getting out of the way and allowing God to take the fight to the enemy says: "One of you routs a thousand, because the Lord your God fights for you, just as he promised" Joshua 23:10. When fighting for your financial life, be smart. Jesus said: "I am sending you out like sheep among wolves. Therefore be as shrewd as snakes and as innocent as doves" Matthew 10:16.

Don't engage the enemy single-handedly. Fight in tandem with God and in God's strength. There are some things the Lord needs for you to do in the spiritual fight. Stay spiritually close to the Lord. Study his word daily. Pray about every decision you make and every action you take. Resist and flee Satan and his temptations, and finally, suit up for battle by putting on the whole armor of God as outlined in Ephesians 6. Pray for and seek the Lord's wisdom and will. Use your head.

Do your research. Talk these decisions over with your spouse and other significant family members. Only after you have done these things make your decision and take action.

12. Move to Safety

When the tragic Tsunami struck in the Indian Ocean on the day after Christmas in 2004 residents of some of the eleven countries affected reported that they had noticed wildlife moving to higher ground during the hours before the tragic event took place. Though they didn't know what was about to happen, those animals had an innate God-given instinct that something terrible was about to take place. In an attempt to survive the upcoming tragedy, they moved to safer surroundings.

Many pet owners report that their pets get edgy or nervous an hour or two before a storm rolls in. What is it that enables a dog to sense the coming storm while humans can't?

Could it be that we are not perceptive enough to feel the atmospheric pressure changes, detect the subtle vibrations, or hear the sub-sonic sounds prior to the coming storm? We don't know all the answers to that question, but we had better be ready to move to higher ground and to safety when crises come into our lives. Use some common sense and learn to sharpen your skills of perception by paying close attention to what is happening all around you. Learn to avoid situations that put you in harm's way. Don't tempt God by being foolish or careless. Keep yourself spiritually, physically, and financially safe. The best thing we can do is to submit our hearts, wills, minds, attitudes, and even our very lives themselves to God and move out of harm's way.

Take charge of your life. Develop the survival mode mentality. Thank God for the gift of the present and for the promise of hope for the future. God's plans for you are good.

God's plans are good even if you are going through a personal disaster in your life right now.

If you are experiencing disaster in your life, learn to trust and rely upon the Lord. Ask him to teach you some of his life-changing principles to get you through and to prepare you for what lies ahead.

13. Contact your Rescuer...the Lord Jesus Christ

A man was once stranded on the roof of his flooded house. As the flood waters continued to rise, he prayed and asked the Lord to save his life. Soon a boat came along with rescuers aboard. The man refused their efforts to rescue him saying: "I can't go with you because the Lord is going to save me." In total bewilderment, they begged him to get in the boat with them but he refused. Soon they left to go and rescue someone else. Next, a helicopter came and lowered a sailor down a rope to rescue the man. Again the man said: "I can't go with you because the Lord is going to save me." They flew away empty-handed.

Later that afternoon as the water crested above his rooftop, yet another helicopter came by and when the rescuer came down on the rope the man said: "I can't go with you because the Lord is going to save me." Reluctantly they flew away, and the man drowned in the flood. When the man arrived in heaven he was mad that he had died and complained to Gabriel that God hadn't answered his prayer and had let him drown. Gabriel was blown away by the man's complaint and replied: "Hey, dummy, don't blame the Lord. It was entirely your fault. The Lord sent three different rescue parties to save your life and you refused them all."

The Lord is your rescuer, but he often works through people to do his work. Both the Lord and the people he has chosen are out there to help you. Your job is to trust the Lord and then pray and seek them out. Don't just sit idly by waiting on something to happen. You may miss your opportunity to be rescued. Pray about your crisis, ask God to guide your plans and to lead you to the right people at the right time, and then take action. In the Old Testament book of Nehemiah 2:4-5, a man by the name of Nehemiah wanted to do something great for the Lord. When asked by King Artaxerxes, "What is it you want?" Nehemiah responded: "Then I prayed to the God of heaven, and I answered the king..." These verses tell us that Nehemiah prayed before taking decisive action. You can do the same thing. Pray about your needs or problems and then follow the Lord's leadership and get up and do something. If you are needing a job don't just sit there waiting for the phone to ring with someone calling to offer you a job. Pray about it, then, get up and get out there and submit numerous applications and attempt to set up some interviews. If you are on the verge of losing your house, take charge of the situation and go talk to all who will listen. Eventually, you will find that person the Lord has put in your path to help you. "He rescues and he saves; he performs signs and wonders in the heavens and on the earth. He has rescued Daniel from the power of the lions" Daniel 6:27.

ETERNAL TRUTH: God Works through People to Answer Many Prayers.

14. MAINTAIN YOUR LIFELINES

"…No man is an island, entire of itself…" wrote John Donne, a Christian, and an English poet of the 17th century. After God created Adam he said: "The Lord God said, 'It is not good for the man to be alone. I will make a helper suitable for him'" Genesis 2:18.

Let's face it…you need other people. We were created to need each other. You are doing yourself a great disservice if you are a loner and don't allow other people to get involved in your life. Some of God's greatest blessings will come only when you allow other people to become involved in your life. Get involved in other people's lives as well. You may be the blessing they are praying for and waiting on.

We are talking about the healthy relationships that would honor God and be beneficial to you. It's called friendship. Someone once said that you would be a wealthy person if, when you died, you had five close friends. How many do you have? You need several. The way to have friends is for you to first be a friend to someone. How does one befriend another person? Strike up a conversation; offer a helping hand; express genuine concern when someone is having a hard day or suffering a loss or undergoing a tragic situation in his or her life. You say: "But I'm afraid to get involved because we live in a world that is full of weird, kinky, and crazy people." You are right; there are a lot of weird, kinky, and crazy people out there. But for every one of those you can find, there are at least 1,000 more who are normal, decent people who need friendships just like you need them. You just have to learn to be a judge of character and know when and where to draw the line on your personal space to keep the wrong kind of people at bay. Don't be a fool. There are lots of people you should avoid and shouldn't have anything to do with. But don't let them prevent you from developing the normal friendships that you need.

It is true that some people have a difficult time relating to God because they had unhealthy or toxic relationships with their fathers or some other male authority figure during their formative years. If you are a person who fits that template, please know that God is not mad at you. God loves you unconditionally. God accepts you as you are, and he really wants to have a positive relationship with you.

Every single one of us had an imperfect biological father. But we do have a PERFECT Heavenly father. Many others had an ungodly biological father. But God is RIGHTEOUS and HOLY. He loves you and would do nothing at all to hurt you. He really means it when he says that he has: "plans to prosper you and not to harm you, plans to give you hope and a future" Jeremiah 29:11.

Your Greatest Lifeline is JESUS

Relational intimacy scares many people. It is the kind of intimacy that allows you to get emotionally close and to love another person. If you are having difficulty being intimate with God, you may find that you also have difficulty being intimate with other people. Please know that Jesus loves you just as you are and he wants you to get to know him in a more personal and intimate way. One of the best ways to get to know him more intimately is to study one chapter of the Gospel of John per day. As you get to know Jesus through his Word, you will begin to like him, and then you will learn to love him, and finally you will learn to trust him and make him a close friend.

Where can one find people to be their friend and find people with whom they can learn to grow closer emotionally? Just look around, they are all around you. Chances are many of them have the same struggles you have and are also looking for a friend. Begin with God, continue in a good church, check out the people with whom you work, and consider the friends you already have. Just look around. They are out there.

Put It All Together

We have come a long way in this chapter outlining financial survival techniques. You and your family must survive your financial crises. God wants to help you survive by teaching you the skills that will enable you to survive and then go far beyond just survival. He wants to teach you how to live an abundant Christian life, a life characterized by intimacy with Jesus and a life filled with the countless blessings he wishes to bestow upon you.

Remember the principle from the beginning of this chapter? Here it is again with a comment to help us understand this timeless truth. Remember this eternal principle: **While God does not always remove our problems, He is willing to guide and equip us in working through them.**

God could have but chose not to remove the crucifixion experience from his son Jesus Christ. However, he did equip him to endure his crucifixion and come out alive on the other side through his Resurrection. After Jesus' Resurrection, he was a conqueror. He conquered the power of sin, Satan, death, hell, and the grave.

This is what God wants for you. He wants you to survive. But he wants you to do far more than to just survive. He wants you to experience and live a life characterized by VICTORY. He wants you to be equipped to handle your next crisis and the next and the next.

Life is filled with series of crises. Look at the heroes of the Bible. They had crises, but they overcame them and were victorious. Some were small and easy to handle. Others were mega sized and almost blew them away. But they survived them and went on to live the victorious life we are discussing. God wants to equip you to be able to handle anything that comes your way. You can not only survive...you can do even better than that. You can be victorious.

Eternal Truth: When our eyes are focused upon Jesus they are not focused upon our problems. When our eyes are focused upon our problems they are not focused upon Jesus.

Refine Your Focus

Have you ever noticed that you can't focus upon two things at once? When our eyes are focused upon Jesus they are not focused upon our problems. Simon Peter discovered this principle when the Lord invited him to walk out to meet him while he was walking across the water (Matthew 14:24-32). Peter climbed out of the boat, took a few steps toward Jesus, and realized that he was doing something no other man besides Jesus had ever done…he was walking on water. He was fine until he began to think about what he was doing. At that moment, he took his eyes off Jesus and focused them upon the wind-driven waves. He became afraid, and suddenly, he plunged beneath the surface. Next, he did something very smart; he cried out to the Lord to save him from drowning. Jesus reached out and picked him up, and let him walk upon the water once again as they walked back to the safety of the boat.

If you have fallen, ask God to pick you back up. He can, and he will, if only you will trust him. Do you need an infusion of God's peace for your life and your family in the middle of your crisis? Focus your eyes and all your faith upon the Lord, not upon your problems. To survive and live a victorious life you have to keep your eyes focused upon Jesus. "You will keep in perfect peace him whose mind is steadfast, because he trusts in you" Isaiah 26:3.

Chapter 10
Taming the Panic Monster

The sailboat sailed upon the high sea. She was a rare sight. An absolute beauty, she was the envy of all who had seen her. As the great ship sailed, the calm day was suddenly punctuated by the sounds of distant thunder. The experienced crew knew that the thunder could be a harbinger of a disastrous storm. Clouds began forming and the winds increased. The sailors couldn't hide their concerns that began to show on their craggy faces. Hardly a word was spoken for deep within they knew what lay ahead. Instinctively, they went about their work maintaining the ship and readying it for the upcoming squall they dreaded.

The first wave of the storm hit. Emerald waves were now breaking over the bow and drenching the wayfarers. Salt stung their eyes as they strained to see the heaving seas through the pungent raindrops. Having hauled in the sails, battened down the hatches, and secured everything on deck, they feared that now they might be in for the ride of their lives. Their fears were realized. Experienced seamen, they had seen both the best and worst that the sea had to offer. This time however, they were afraid they had entered a deadly storm. Thoughts raced through their minds like incessant lightning bolts that flashed throughout the sky. Their thoughts centered on their families, their wives, children, and parents. The older sailors thought about their grandchildren and whether they would ever see them again. They knew that this was the big one and while they had seen rough seas and huge storms before, none had seen anything so powerful as this.

Wicked torrents of rains were driving with such force they could hardly keep their eyes opened. Experienced crewmen had already lashed themselves to the mast or the railings to keep from being swept overboard. The plebes had even caught on to this trick and had tied off. Then it happened. The mast snapped like a twig under the foot of a hunter. It was blown into the sea and the crew now focused on nothing but raw survival. Communication with one another was impossible because of the horrific hurricane-like winds. Their hearts gripped by panic, the crew was terrified. Never in their lives had they witnessed such a fierce storm. By now, each man had come to the bone-chilling conclusion that this day would likely be his very last.

One sailor was obsessed with the thought of the captain's life. So driven to know the truth and so enthralled with emotion, the normally vociferous but now deafeningly quite man simply had to know about their captain. Had he been swept overboard and drowned? Had he tied himself to the main mast and been killed when it was flung into the sea? It was incomprehensible that he was missing, for he was a master sailor who never made mistakes. Peter had to know. He untied himself and clawed his way across the rolling and heaving deck to one of the hatches to go below to look for his captain. As he fell down the stairs he spotted what appeared to be a body silhouetted by a lightning flash in the dark cabin. Tumbling over to the lifeless image he was incredulous when he realized that it was the captain and that he was sound asleep. Peter shook him and he awakened. Peter shouted to him: "Don't you care if we drown?" The Master sailor arose, climbed up on deck, and rebuked the wind and waves as he said: "Peace, be still!" The wind and waves vanished and the sea became completely still.

The sailors were stupefied. They had just witnessed the impossible. Merely five seconds earlier they faced certain death but now the storm was gone. Jesus broke the silence by asking: "Why are you so afraid? Do you still have no faith?" They were terrified and asked each other, "Who is this? Even the wind and the waves obey him!" The words of Jesus are taken from Mark 4:39-40, Matthew 8:23-27, Luke 8:22-25. Read them for yourself.

ETERNAL TRUTH: It is safer within the will of God in a dangerous place than in a safe place outside God's will.

America was like a storm-tossed ship in 2008 and 2009. Sailing on a wild and unforgiving economic sea threatened her very survival. What does the future hold for America? No one except God himself knows the answer to that question. Almost everyone agrees that the basic economic fundamentals have changed and will continue to change over the next several years. You can anticipate much greater deficit spending; borrowed billions upon hundreds of billions of dollars from China and other sources; higher taxes; and socio-political maneuvering. Add the threat of predicted probable terrorist attacks upon our homeland, and it becomes rather obvious that the storm is not over. Some of the roughest seas ever sailed may lay ahead for our nation and her people. Get ready, for if you live in America, you will be sailing on those same uncharted seas.

What will the future hold for you and your family? "Are there things I can do to help me prepare for the future and tame the panic monster?" you ask. Only God knows the future, but spiritual wisdom suggests that there are several things you can do to better prepare yourself and your family for the events that lay ahead for our country.

Misplaced Faith

In a state of panic, many people are tempted to place their faith in any one or more of the following: the government, their money, their wealth, their 401(k)s, the stock market, the economy, Social Security, politicians, their financial planner, themselves, or any number of other things. The point is this: you can trust any of these things or anything else you choose to trust. But there is ample evidence that you will be disappointed again and again and again.

Do you remember the Bernard Madoff scandal? His $50 billion investment ponzi scheme collapsed and thousands of high-dollar investors lost everything they had. One investor, Rene-Thierry Magon de la Villehuchet, the co-founder of a firm that lost $1.5 billion in the scandal, committed suicide in his New York apartment. Madoff's ponzi scheme reminds one of America's Social Security program. Many people are placing their financial faith for the future in their ability to receive a monthly check from the government. Unfortunately, Social Security is seen by most experts as a program that is unsustainable. It is operated in a virtually identical fashion to the Madoff ponzi scheme. The major difference is that it is much larger. Many experts warn people not to tie their total retirement to that star, for at some future point, it will not be able to sustain itself in its present form.

Wall Street greed has done much to decimate your retirement accounts. If you have several years remaining before your projected retirement, your 401(k)s may be able to build back much of their values. However, once they build back, who is to say that another economic crisis couldn't come along and devastate them once again? With all this uncertainty, where can one go and who can one trust?

ETERNAL TRUTH: YOU CAN OVERCOME PANIC BY PLACING YOUR FAITH IN JESUS

1. JESUS CAN REPLACE YOUR UNCERTAINTIES WITH CERTAINTY

In the middle of financial panic and economic upheaval, there is but one unchanging force in the entire universe. He is the only one worthy of your faith. He has never let anyone down and he will always be there to guide and bless you. "Jesus Christ is the same yesterday and today and forever" Hebrews 13:8.

2. JESUS CAN REPLACE YOUR FEARS WITH FAITH

There is a lot of fear in America and the world today. Fear is based largely upon uncertainty…more specifically, uncertainty about the future. While this uncertainty hasn't reached the panicked proportions of the Great Depression, we still do not know the ramifications it will have on our futures. Jesus not only knows the future, he also holds the future in his hand. God gives us great wisdom and guidance about both the present and the future: "When I am afraid, I will trust in you" Psalm 56:3. "For God did not given us a spirit of timidity; but a spirit of power, of love and of self-discipline" 2 Timothy 1:7. God wants to replace your fear with faith.

3. JESUS CAN REPLACE YOUR ANXIETY WITH CONFIDENCE

God knows every minute detail about everything you are experiencing right now. He is able and willing to help you cope with everything in your life. "Do not be anxious about anything, but in everything, by prayer and petition, with thanksgiving, present your requests to God" Philippians 4:6. You can have confidence in the future. You can have it by placing your faith in Jesus and allowing him to replace your anxiety with confidence.

4. Jesus Can Replace Your Bondage with Freedom

The terrible institution of slavery has existed for thousands of years. It existed during the time Jesus walked the earth. Unfortunately, it still exists today. Human bondage is one of the gravest of all injustices ever perpetrated upon mankind. Unfortunately, many Americans live in one of the many forms of spiritual bondage today. Jesus came to set us free from both spiritual and other forms of bondage. "For you did not receive a spirit that makes you a slave again to fear, but you received the Spirit of sonship" Romans 8:15.

Christians have been granted "sonship" into God's family. Sonship grants us a certain status with God. It is as if we have been adopted into God's family and have become heirs alongside Jesus Christ. Paul knew about ancient Roman adoption laws when he was led of the Holy Spirit to write that verse. An adopted child was protected by legal rights that were actually much stronger than the laws governing natural sonship. A natural born son could be disinherited from his father's estate for any reason his father might choose. However, an adopted son could not be disinherited for any reason, period. In biblical times, adoption was actually stronger than natural sonship. When Paul wrote that Christians have "received the Spirit of sonship," he was revealing to us the fact that Christians have a superior standing with God and that adoption into God's family is permanent. Sin and anything outside the realm of faith in Jesus can lead to bondage. Jesus replaces our former bondage to a life of sin with a life of freedom and sonship.

We in America cherish freedom. We are blessed to enjoy the freedom that was granted by God and bequeathed by our forefathers. Almost 1,700 years before America declared her independence; the Bible spoke the wonderful truth that believers have been made free. "Then you will know the truth, and the truth will set you free" John 8:32. And, "So if the Son sets you free, you will be free indeed" John 8:36. Will you allow Jesus to set you free from spiritual and material bondage?

5. Jesus Can Replace Your Fears with Perfect Love

"There is no fear in love. But perfect love drives out fear, because fear has to do with punishment. The one who fears is not made perfect in love" 1 John 4:18. As we learn to put our trust in Jesus our fears become less important. Fears eventually fade away and are replaced by a growing faith and confidence in him. The more you fear, the harder it is to love God. The more you love God, the harder it is to fear. Fears are based in uncertainty. Uncertainties are cured by faith in Jesus.

ETERNAL TRUTH: The more you fear, the harder it is to love God. The more you love God, the harder it is to fear.

LEARN TO ASK THE RIGHT QUESTIONS

One of the most important questions you need to ask yourself during a time of crisis is this: "God, what would you have me to learn as a result of going through this crisis?" The valuable lessons learned during times of crisis have the potential to change our understanding, our motivation, our faith, our attitudes, our thinking, and our way of life. Crises have the potential to change our lives by redirecting our outlooks and instilling principles that will guide us throughout the rest of our lives. Seize the moment. Don't let this life-changing opportunity slip through your fingers like grains of sand. Don't waste a great opportunity for spiritual growth.

SOME STORMS ARE NECESSARY IN LIFE

Life's storms, crises, and tough times are usually the best vehicles to force us to trust God and to grow in our faith.

THE TWO MAJOR OPTIONS THAT ARE AVAILABLE

There are many options available to you at this time of crisis. However, these can be reduced to the two most basic options anyone can have at this time.

1. You may trust the Lord to get you through.

2. You may trust someone or something else and attempt to make a go of it without God.

The choice is a no brainer. If you trust the Lord, learn from him, and rise up out of the drowning waters you can sail on to victory. Without the God, your ultimate eternal destiny will be panic and terror.

WHAT MAY HAPPEN IF I DON'T PLACE MY TRUST IN JESUS?

Not trusting in God can lead one to other options; none of which is good.

1. You May Live your Life Apart from God

Millions are doing this and are quite materially successful without God. You can be materially successful yet be spiritually bankrupt. Enjoy your success now because it is all you will ever have or enjoy. When your life is over and you exit this earth to meet the Lord, you will be spiritually impoverished. "Then I will tell them plainly, 'I never knew you. Away from me, you evildoers!'" Matthew 7:23.

2. You May Suffer From Sheer Panic

If you assume that Jesus is not in control the best option you have left is to trust in yourself. The outcome of you against the world leads to certain defeat for you. The absolute worst things you can possibly do are to NOT trust in the Lord and to PANIC.

3. You May Suffer From Spiritual Anemia

If you miss these unprecedented opportunities to put your faith and trust in the Lord you may grow spiritually weak. Opportune times like these are optimal growth opportunities, don't miss them. Do you know that Jesus could snap his fingers and correct the world's global economy just as he quieted the storm? Why, he wouldn't even have to snap his fingers…he could merely think the thought and it would be corrected. Then why doesn't he do just that? Stop the storm? The same reason he doesn't put everyone into a $1,000,000 dollar home with a new Ferrari and a Hummer in the garage and a bank account with a $5,000,000 balance. He wants you to work for it. Plus, he knows that many who enjoy that much prosperity can't handle it and they prove that they can't handle it by boxing God out of their lives.

4. You May Underestimate God's Power

Jesus' disciples had underestimated his power. They knew him intimately but didn't know just how powerful he was. Could the same tendency to underestimate God's power be true of you and other Christians today? Absolutely. All Christians face the temptation to underestimate God's power. If Jesus could calm the storm that threatened the lives of he and his disciples; if he could simply speak and the winds and waves obey him; if he could rebuke the storm and make it stop, he can do the same and more for you and your family as you find yourselves within the grip of your personal financial storm.

Again, there are many options available to you at this time of crisis. Do yourself a gigantic favor and make the deliberate choice to trust the Lord to get you through.

LIFE GOES ON DURING TIMES OF PANIC

Read a Scripture verse that was written during a time of war. "For I know the plans I have for you, declares the LORD, plans to prosper you and not to harm you, plans to give you hope and a future" Jeremiah 29:11. This verse was written during a major crisis…war. The people to whom it was written were living in panic mode. Judah, the Southern Kingdom of Israel, had been invaded by King Nebuchadnezzar of Babylon. Babylon had become the new world power and had defeated Assyria in 612 BC and Egypt in 605 BC. Now, she was invading tiny Judah. Judah would experience three Babylonian invasions. They happened in 605, 597, 586 BC. Each time they were invaded, the Babylonians deported thousands of Jews and exiled them as captives to Babylon.

God was the force behind the Babylonian invasion and captivity. He had warned Israel that unless they repented they would be punished for their sins. What was Israel's sin? They had tolerated a series of wicked, ungodly kings who turned them away from God to idol worship. God used Babylon's King Nebuchadnezzar, and his forced exile to get Israel's attention in order to bring them back to obedience and faithfulness to him. God uses a prophet named Jeremiah to speak to the people of Judah. He spoke both to the Jews living in Babylon and those still living in Jerusalem. Jeremiah was an awesome prophet of God who was still living in Jerusalem when God led him to write his book of prophecy to the exiles in Babylon. When Jeremiah wrote this verse, it was part of a letter he had written to his fellow Jews who were in exile in Babylon. That letter is recorded in Jeremiah 29:4-23. This beautiful verse was sent by God to his people during a time of crisis and panic. The verse was meant to encourage, assure, invigorate, bless, give hope, and communicate God's love, care, and plans. If you study the letter in its entirety you will find that God identifies himself as the one who initiated exile, and instructed the exiles to seek peace and prosperity:

"This is what the Lord Almighty, the God of Israel, says to all those I carried into exile from Jerusalem to Babylon: 'Build houses and settle down; plant gardens and eat what they produce. Marry and have sons and daughters; find wives for your sons and give your daughters in marriage, so that they too may have sons and daughters. Increase in number there; do not decrease. Also, seek the peace and prosperity of the city to which I have carried you into exile. Pray to the Lord for it, because if it prospers, you too will prosper" Jeremiah 29:4-7.

Practical observations from this passage that you may apply to your financial situation:

1. God was very much in control of the situation.

2. God caused their exile in order to draw his people back to him.

3. God wanted to bless his people in spite of the crisis they were experiencing.

4. God told them to expect to be there for a while.

5. God instructed them to build, plant, and have children and grandchildren.

6. God told them to seek prosperity.

7. God told them to pray for the pagan nation who had enslaved them.

Conclusions from this passage:
1. Trust in the Lord.

2. Life goes on during a crisis.

3. Don't panic.

"For I know the plans I have for you, declares the LORD, plans to prosper you and not to harm you, plans to give you hope and a future" Jeremiah 29:11. This verse may have much more meaning for you since you now have some background information. God gave this promise to you to enable you to have confidence and renewed faith in him. What an awesome God we serve.

PUT IT ALL TOGETHER

We started this chapter with the mother of all storms. We end it with an important question. Why was Jesus taking a nap in the middle of the storm? Before you read any further, how would you like to answer that question for yourself? Jesus could have kept the storm from scaring his disciples half to death. Instead, he chose to take a nap. Why was he so insensitive to their needs? Why didn't he rebuke the storm before it blew in and brought panic to his friends. The answer: he knew that they needed to benefit from the experience they were about to have. He knew that it would make them grow in their faith and teach them a valuable lesson about trusting in their Lord. Besides being tired and needing a nap, Jesus knew that his disciples needed to grow in their faith.

Fortunately for us, Jesus is not going to make our economic storms disappear. He is so powerful that he could simply snap his fingers, or think the thought, and in a mere instant could upright America's floundering economy. He could think the thought and make you rich. However, one reason he may have chosen to allow us to experience this crisis is to cause us to grow. Could it be that he is also allowing us to experience this crisis in order to humble us and to cause us to repent and come back to him? God's word says that he will judge the nations. Might it be that these things are happening as a form of judgment upon America and the greater world population at large in order to bring the attention of the world back to him? Only God himself knows the answer to these questions but if it is his judgment he is applying it out of such deep love as to draw us back to him.

America's financial storm has widened to worldwide proportions. World stock and investment markets have fallen dramatically. In addition, plummeting currency values and morale is literally shaking the foundations of many of the peoples of the U.S. and the world. The financial storm has sunk many people's hopes and dreams, and no one can accurately predict its long-term impact.

During one three week period in October 2008 Americans lost some two trillion dollars of their 401K retirement accounts. U.S. Stock Market plunges of 300-500 to point drops per trading day were common as the market searched for a bottom. Could the economic downturn ultimately sink our economy, and possibly even become so devastating that it could sink our country, bring global financial ruin, or worldwide economic collapse? That is doubtful. However, financial security is teetering and is on the verge of disappearing for millions of Americans. It has already disappeared for some, while others never had it at all. America and the world are changing. Many feel that we are being stripped of our basic heritage including our beliefs, our faith, our morality, our society, our decency, and now our financial security.

But what are you to do and where are you to turn? There are many answers to these questions. But the real solution is Jesus. He can enable you to overcome panic and fear. He and he alone can teach you how to not only survive, but how to excel and to reach your God-given potential. He can instill and inspire personal responsibility, family values and morals, and can teach you to grow through the trials that lie ahead.

These are exciting times for they hold our future, a future fraught with opportunity to grow, mature and to succeed. Some wag once said: "You won't get out of this world alive." He was right and he was wrong. Even Christians will die, but they will get out of this world alive and will live with Jesus in heaven forever. "But those who hope in the Lord will renew their strength. They will soar on wings like eagles; they will run, and not be weary, and they will walk, and not be faint" Isaiah 40:31. Learn to place your faith and trust in God. Learn to wait upon him and listen for his leadings. Learn from the thousands of answers awaiting you within his Word, the Bible. Wait upon the Lord, be renewed, and fly with the eagles. God has something good in store for you.

A Suggested Prayer to Pray, to Meditate Upon, and to Incorporate Into your Life:

Lord, I want to be still and know that you are God. I am willing to listen to you and discover your will for my life. I am willing to place my faith in you and in you alone. I renounce my faith in my financial holdings, real estate, retirement accounts, and yes, even my faith in government. I am willing to put my faith in you, and I am willing to learn the lessons you want me to learn in order to bring me into a more intimate personal relationship with Jesus Christ, Amen.

Chapter 11
Taming the Debt Monster

DREAM A LITTLE

Freedom from debt brings unbelievable freedom! Imagine how you would feel if you could walk up to the airport ticket counter, check your luggage, and pick up boarding passes for a Caribbean vacation for you and your family knowing that your trip had already been paid for because you had the cash reserves to pay for your trip. If that is a little too dramatic, imagine walking into your favorite grocery store and buying a cart filled with anything you wanted without any concern about how much it was going to cost. You swipe your debit card and walk out with unbridled confidence with your head held high. Imagine going clothes shopping for your family and being able to spend hundreds of dollars without feeling the least bit guilty? Again, you swipe your debit card and leave the mall feeling wonderful about your day. What would it feel like to be able to go into your favorite electronics store and pick out a new top-of-the-line big screen TV without even flinching? Those dreams are realities for many people and the reasons they can do these things may surprise you. It is not that they are rich. One of the reasons they could go to these places and make their purchases is that they are entirely out of debt. Being debt free brings a degree of freedom like you wouldn't believe. Once again, you can enjoy spending your money without feeling the least bit guilty.

THE GREATEST FINANCIAL BURDEN FOR AMERICANS IS DEBT

The Federal Reserve estimates that Americans are carrying approximately $1 trillion in debt. This estimate is for what is called revolving consumer debt, most of which is credit card debt. The $1 trillion dollar debt does not include mortgages. People's largest debt, their home mortgage, is not the problem. The problem is the open lines of credit they maintain. Open lines of credit include credit cards and home equity loans. The biggest problem is credit cards. Government estimates reveal that the average credit card debt in America is just over $4,000 per person, or $8,000 per family. This is precisely the reason people have to watch what they buy in the grocery, clothing, and electronics stores. In addition to credit cards many people are up to their eyeballs in debt through the little invention called the Home Equity Line of Credit. Couple this with credit card debt and it is easy to see why many people have this nervous feeling in the pits of their stomachs. Their problem is twofold: First is the fact that they allow themselves to get into debt in the first place. Second is the fact that they keep spending and charging to credit cards like there is no tomorrow.

DEBT IS A FORM OF SLAVERY

If you were approached by a stranger who walked up and demanded you give up your rights and privileges and become their personal slave you would call the police and have them arrested for harassment. The sad fact is that many of your friends and relatives have become enslaved by their debts. We have been conditioned to have insatiable appetites for food, clothing, flashy cars, entertainment, jewelry, travel, electronics, and about anything else you can imagine. We have developed attitudes of greed. We live in a credit-driven nation whose economy is experiencing economic upheaval because of our voracious appetites for things and spending. Why would anyone willingly allow someone else to gain control over them? It makes absolutely no sense at all, does it?

One of the most striking features of the $700 billion TARP bailout of October 2008 was the fact that Congress stated that they wanted to: "get the credit markets flowing again." Hello. We are a credit-driven nation with an estimated $60 trillion debt obligation. (Including the obligations intended for future funding of government entitlement programs such as Social Security, Medicare, and Medicaid.) We just witnessed Congress and President Bush hurriedly ram through a $700 billion bailout bill followed by President Obama's $787 billion American Recovery and Reinvestment Act of 2009. Both bills were passed against the wishes of the majority of the American people. We were told that as a nation we can "spend our way out of debt." Are we crazy or what? Something really is wrong with this picture. This concept is totally devoid of logic. We are in trouble and we will be in trouble for the next several generations. Our grandchildren and great grandchildren will be the ones who will suffer the most because of the major consequences of our nation's reckless borrowing and overspending. It has been estimated that America is borrowing 46 cents of every dollar spent in 2009, and that America's national debt will consume 82% of our economy by 2019.

Learn from Uncle Sam

Please don't attempt to "spend your way out of debt," with your own personal finances. You will likely spend your way into bankruptcy court, and the government will not be there to bail you out from your indebtedness. One of the most puzzling things about all of this is that we are willing to allow some of the very people (both political parties share the blame,) who were responsible for creating our problems to be the ones to try and fix them.

It hurts to have to include the following but it is true. When it comes to your personal finances take a good look at our federal government's examples on budgeting, spending, borrowing, deficit spending, financial appropriations, and Washington DC's overall approach to money and finances, and do just the opposite. If you were owner of a business or a corporation and ran your affairs in exactly the same manner as our federal government, you would be imprisoned for the shenanigans you pulled off.

SHINY NEW CREDIT CARD

Credit card interest rates can reach a whopping 35% Annual Percentage Rate (APR) for some people. Home equity loans usually come with a lower interest rate, ranging from 8-15%. To understand the APR, imagine that you have a shiny new credit card carrying a $10,000 balance at 24% interest. The interest on that $10,000 balance for one year would equal: $2,400. That means that if you could maintain an exact monthly balance of $10,000 for four years, your principal amount owed would be $10,000 plus the $9,600 interest you will have paid over those four years would equal $19,600. Did you get that? In four years you will have paid $9,600 in interest alone. Just think what you could do with $9,600? Can you imagine that your $10,000 debt would have nearly doubled to $19,600 in just four years?

Imagine the same scenario if someone were carrying a total balance of $30,000 spread over several cards for the same four years. Their total interest charges for four years would be a whopping $38,400. Insane isn't it? Didn't the Lord have something very important to say about the rich ruling over the poor, and the borrower being a servant to the lender? Yes, it was in Proverbs 22:7.

I CAN GET OUT OF DEBT

There is hope for you. "How do I go about getting out of debt, becoming debt-free, and taming the debt monster if I owe several thousand dollars in credit card debt," you ask? The best answer is a financial strategy created by Dave Ramsey, as outlined in his book: ***Total Money Makeover***, published by Thomas Nelson in 2003. Ramsey is on the cutting-edge of the Christian financial reform movement. Dave developed a plan that he calls the "Debt Snowball." His plan is a straight-forward approach. When followed as it was designed; Dave's plan will provide splendid results for anyone, regardless of the size of their credit card debt. The debt snowball enables you to pay off all your credit card debts with a very simple and proven approach.

You may start Dave's plan by saving $1,000 in cash to fully-fund your emergency spending fund. No cheating please. You will need to have this in reserve in the likely event that spending emergencies arise. Having this fund will keep you from having to charge anything back to a credit card. Once you have saved the $1,000 cash and deposited it in the bank, you are ready to begin paying off your credit cards.

Begin with your credit card that has the smallest balance. Concentrate your greatest efforts toward paying it off completely. At the same time you are paying it off you continue to make the minimum monthly payments on all your remaining credit cards. For example, you want to pay off your Consolidated National Bank Card with a $1,100 balance first. After making the minimum payments on all your other cards, pay all the money you possibly can toward paying off your Consolidated card. Pay it off as soon as possible. Continue doing this month by month until you have your Consolidated card paid down to a zero balance.

Oh, I did fail to mention something? This is very important. While you are paying off your credit card debts, you need to stop using your credit cards, period. Add no more to the debts you are paying off. If you keep adding more debt to what you already have you are shooting yourself in the foot...and that hurts.

So how do I stop spending when I am in the habit of spending tons of money with my credit cards? Ramsey has this huge pair of scissors that he uses to perform "plastic surgery." You may want to call your family together, explain what you and your spouse have agreed to do, and in ceremonious fashion take out your scissors and cut your credit cards in half. This says two things to your family: you are serious about getting out of debt, and you have just made a commitment not to use your credit cards again.

Some people with a lot less resolve and a lot less flair freeze their credit cards in containers full of water until they become encased in blocks of ice. They then keep the frozen cards in the freezer where they can't be used too easily. However, be careful when preparing dinner lest you accidentally serve up a dish of credit card casserole.

The theory of freezing your credit cards is that you will have to think about a spending decision before you commit to it. Also, at least you will have to thaw the block of ice before you can charge anything. Pretty good plan but it has a flaw: the card is still there and available for you to use. Even if frozen within a block of ice, the temptation to retrieve it from the freezer and go shopping will be too great for some people. The scissors route is for the really serious-minded people among us. It's like quitting cold-turkey. Once you have used the scissors, you have made a commitment and you can't go back.

Now that you have Consolidated paid off, celebrate. Get your spouse and the kids together and go out to your favorite restaurant. Just remember to pay cash. You have just won a significant victory. You have scored a touchdown and are now ahead in the game. Don't look back, keep forging ahead and score another. Next, take on your Amalgamated Credit card. Knock it out in the same manner, putting all you possibly can toward paying it off while making minimum payments on all the others. When Amalgamated is zeroed out, go to the Acme credit card, and then to your final credit card. When you finish this you will have taken a mega step into your secure financial future. This method works. There is not a better method available for you to rid yourself from credit card debt.

The "Debt Snowball's" success for you will be contingent upon three things. First, fully-fund your $1,000 emergency fund and put the cash in the bank. Second, you must stop charging to your credit cards. Third, you must make the commitment to pay them off and stop at nothing until they are all zeroed out. This plan has enabled some people to pay off credit card debts that would stagger the imagination. It is nothing for a couple to pay off a $20,000 debt using Dave's "Debt Snowball." What a weird name? Well it's not weird when you understand the concept. As a snowball rolls down a snowy hill it gets bigger and bigger and builds momentum as it rolls. As you begin paying off your credit cards you gain bigger and bigger chunks of control of your life. As you continue, you gain momentum. Keep going until you have paid off all your cards and you are the winner. You are now debt free.

Before you attempt to begin this journey, get your spouse and family on board with the concept of getting out of debt. Talk this over with them and show them how it will benefit every one of them and how it will bring your family financial freedom.

Sudden Rush of Euphoria

Warning: as you go through the plan you suddenly realize that you are beginning take charge of your financial life again. When this happens, and it will, you will get this sudden rush of euphoria. This rush comes from the fact that you are beginning to experience freedom from debt. Some people really get into it and take an extra job delivering pizzas, newspapers, or something part time to put more money toward the debts. Others, who have enough on their plates already decide to cut their living expenses drastically by eating at home 95% of the time, by skipping the movies, skipping a cruise, brown bagging their lunch to work, selling their jewelry, having a garage sale, or selling stuff on the Internet. Take all that extra cash you earn and apply it to your credit card debt. It will help you get out even quicker.

What About my Other Debts?

Almost everyone will still owe for a home mortgage, a car payment or two, college loans, kid's braces, and possibly even a home equity line of credit. What does one do with these? Work toward paying them all off in exactly the same way you paid off your credit card debts. Start with the smallest and work toward the largest. By now you are well on your way to being totally debt-free. It will take some time but one day you will make it.

It is safe to say that you will never get your finances under control and will never show your money who's boss until you zero out your credit card debts and transform your thinking about credit cards and debt in general. For some, taming this money monster may be the hardest thing you have ever attempted to do. You can do it. Literally thousands upon thousands have used this method successfully and are now debt-free. You can take back control of your life. Stop charging to credit cards.

Transition to Cash

Pay cash for everything. It is truly liberating to be debt-free. You can shop for groceries, clothes, electronics, a new car, or almost anything else you want. This time you are shopping without two of your old shopping companions: fear and guilt. You no longer have to charge anything; you now have the cash to pay for it. Sure, it will require some adjustments in your lifestyle for a while. Sure, it will take a lot of sacrifice and doing without. But it will be worth it. You don't really want to spend the rest of your life deeply in debt. The object is to get ahead, not fall further behind. Now is the time for you to decide to get out of debt. You can stop using your credit cards and pay them down to a zero balance.

One of the Greatest Challenges in History

Famed polar explorer Sir Ernest Shackleton wrote this ad that appeared in a London newspaper in 1900. He later said: "It seemed as though all the men in Great Britain were determined to accompany me, the response was so overwhelming."

Below is a copy of Shackleton's actual ad:

Men Wanted for Hazardous Journey
Small wages, bitter cold, long months of complete darkness, constant danger, safe return doubtful. Honor and recognition in case of success.————-
Ernest Shackleton 1.

Accept the Challenge

You can take back control of your life. Stop charging to Credit Cards. Start paying cash for everything. It is truly liberating to be debt-free. With the Lord's help you can do it. It will be tough when you begin having those credit card withdrawal symptoms, but you can handle it. You are tougher than you think.

For more excellent strategies on becoming free of debt and living a debt-free life, check out Dave Ramsey's: **Total Money Makeover**, Thomas Nelson, 2003. For this and other resources visit: www.daveramsey.com and www.christianretirement.com

1. Ernest Shackleton's ad from 1900 in book: **The 100 Greatest Advertisements**, by Julian Lewis Clark, 1959.

Chapter 12
Taming the Payday Monster

The 10/90 Principle…Pay Yourself First

Let me introduce you to a **RADICAL PRINCIPAL**…The 10/90 Principle. Pay yourself 10% of your income before paying any of your bills. Live off the remaining 90%. Why? If you are not paying yourself first, you are merely working for everyone else. You have placed yourself in a form of financial bondage…financial slavery. You earned the money. It belongs to YOU. Why should you pay out all your hard-earned money to those who provide your mortgage, credit cards, auto loan, utilities, cell phone, gasoline, clothing, insurance, and food? Why should they get all your money? Once you learn and understand this principle you may decide not to spend all your money for the goods and services you enjoy. You may decide to keep at least 10% for yourself.

Paying yourself first is radical, and sounds foreign or totally strange, if not impossible. It will cause some to say: "That's a good idea for some people, but not for me." Read on, for you may become convinced that this is for you. There are many people who wish that someone had shared this wisdom with them when they were in their younger years because they could have been rich today.

Admittedly, it may take a lot of work and time before you can fully incorporate the **Pay Yourself First Principle** into your financial life. You are probably like almost everyone else you know in that your expenses require pretty much everything you bring home in your paycheck. The fact is that almost everyone either lives up or down to the level of their take home pay. Whether you bring home $50,000 or $500,000 a year you will tend to live on it all. Many people who bring home $50,000 dollars a year and are always out of money just like some people who bring home $5,000,000 a year that are always out of money. Impossible. How can this be? It's simple; people adjust their lifestyles up or down to the amount of money they have available to spend. The multi-millionaire will spend his money on big houses, fancy cars, fine jewelry, yachts, extravagant vacations, second homes at the beach, and so forth. He may still have just as much trouble as you trying to make payments on all his extravagances. What's more, the guy may not have a dime in savings; he spends it all. You say: "I sure would like to try my hand at living on $5,000,000 a year. I know that I could do better." Some lottery winners have been given the unexpected chance to do just that and blew their opportunity. A few even end up far worse off than they have ever been. Money was not the answer to their problems, in fact, money created even more problems for them.

PERSONAL ACTION ITEM

Deliberately adjust your lifestyle to a level where you can pay yourself 10% of your take home pay BEFORE paying all of your living expenses. This means that you will need to adjust your finances so that you may live on the remaining 90% of your take home pay. Save or invest that 10% that you are paying yourself. For example: you are bringing home $100,000 per year and you want to enact the Pay Yourself First Principle. Where do you begin? First you save or invest 10% or a total of $10,000 of that $100,000 take home pay you receive per year. Next, you adjust your lifestyle to live on $90,000 per year instead of the $100,000 you once lived on. "That will be the toughest thing I have ever done," you say. Probably so, but just consider how much would you have at the end of a ten year period…10 years X $10,000 per year equals $100,000 right? Wrong. You would have the $100,000 PLUS what it has earned. Depending upon the type of investments you choose, you could have something in the range of $105,000—$200,000 + at the end of those ten years. "You are kidding me, right?" It's true that $10,000 a year for ten years will yield well over $100,000. Can you handle that? Knowing that tends to make you want to do without a few trips to your favorite fast food hangout, buy a fewer less DVDs, order less home-delivered pizza, drive your car a couple of years longer, go on a less expensive vacation, and start saving some money to invest.

Suppose that you earn $100,000 a year and you begin the practice of paying yourself first at age 30 and continue to pay yourself a minimum of 10% of your income until age 65. What kind of retirement nest egg could you build with that? Even if your income remained frozen at $100,000 per year for 35 years you still will have saved a minimum of $350,000 in principle. Not to mention the interest, earnings, or dividends that it will have earned. What you have done is you have just set yourself up to win with an investment that will likely be worth several million dollars when you retire at age 65. Imagine what it would be if you based it upon an even greater amount. Say you are earning $250,000 to $500,000 per year and do the same 10% with that; where would you be financially at age 65?

STARK REALITY

How many people do you know who have retired after working 40-plus years and never paid themselves a dime? I know many. Over one's working lifetime the average person can expect to earn well over one million dollars. Why, even if a person was locked in to an income level of $40,000 per year they would earn $1,600,000 over a period of 40 years. If you were locked in at $80,000 per year for 40 years you would earn $3,200,000. Some of you will earn many times that amount over your lifetimes.

What will you have to show for it when you retire at age 65 or 70? Wouldn't it be tragic for you to have earned a few million dollars over your working lifetime and then have nothing much to show for it? Countless numbers of people have retired with nothing but a dependence upon the government to take care of them through Social Security and Medicare.

Don't fall into that trap. Refuse to spend everything you earn. Pay yourself first and then live off the remaining 90% of your take home pay. But you may say: "I really would like to try that but I just can't do it right now. I need every penny I make just to make ends meet." There is an answer to that cop out…the answer lies in your priorities. You can do it, but you will just need to start making some adjustments to your lifestyle.

Start today by talking to your spouse and agree to start at some level. You could begin by paying yourself first with as little as $10.00 per week. Between the two of you, this can be done with just a little effort. Instead of buying a couple of cans of soda per day at work for $1.00 a pop, drink bottled water that you bring from home, the water you bottle from your kitchen tap, not the $3.00 a bottle imported swamp water from the melting glaciers in the Russian tundra.

Once you have started the process of living on less begin to scale up to $25, then $50, and then even $100 dollars per week. Do these steps until you reach your 10% goal or more. Teach this principle to your kids. Start with them as soon as they are able to count and to understand the concept of money and pay as a reward for work. Be creative with your teens because this concept will blow their minds. They will find that NONE of their friends are doing this. Most will have never heard of saving any amount of their money. Motivate them. Help them begin saving. Teach them the value of paying themselves first. Just get them started. One thing is for sure. They may NEVER start practicing this concept unless you model it for them. Everyone has monthly bills and everyone has a certain amount of money that they live on. Your family has decided to do things a little differently. You have decided to take charge of your lives by saving for your futures, and have taken a major step in showing your money who's boss.

Pay yourself first. Pay yourself before paying any of your bills. Admittedly, it sounds radical. It is a foreign concept to at least nine out of ten Americans. It may sound strange or even impossible…but it works. If you choose not to pay yourself first, then best wishes, because you are going to need them.

What do I do with the Money I pay Myself?

You have many options available for the money you pay yourself. First, the worst option is to spend it. Other poor options include: doing nothing with it, stashing it under your mattress, putting it in a safe in your basement, parking it in a safe deposit box in your bank, asking your brother-in-law to keep it safe for you, and a few other nonsensical ideas. You will have to decide which option is best for you and your family.

You Can Retire as a Millionaire

One of the best options will be for you to invest your money and allow it to have a chance to multiply. There are various ways you can invest your money. A few of the most common ways are listed below. No matter where you choose to invest your money there will be some risk involved. This section highlights some of the options that are available. It is not my intention to make any financial recommendations. You will need to make those decisions for yourself. Note: many have benefitted from using a qualified financial advisor to guide them in making informed investment decisions.

We witnessed a meltdown of the stock market in 2008-2009, and many people lost significant portions of their investments (40-60% or more.) Risk is the twin of investment. Any time you place your money in the marketplace in an attempt to have it grow, there is risk. Generally speaking, the lower the degree of risk, the lower the rate of potential returns on your money and the higher the degree of risk, the higher the rate of potential returns on your money.

Be aware that no one can guarantee growth in your investment portfolio, and that no one can predict future tax consequences. However, many experts say that investing is still a better alternative than merely stashing your money in a shoe box and placing it in a closet in your house or putting it in a low-interest CD.

INVEST THE 10% YOU PAY YOURSELF

Take personal responsibility for your financial future by investing the 10% you are paying yourself. There are many possibilities for your consideration; a few of which are outlined below. Remember to do your homework before you invest any of your money. Finally, only invest with highly reputable company.

401(k)s

Perhaps the easiest way to pay yourself first is through automatic deductions from your paycheck. Once you begin contributing to this program and adjust your budget accordingly, you will find that you won't miss the money you would have taken home in your paycheck. In some instances, because of taxes, your take home pay could actually be greater once you begin contributing a percentage of your income. Many employers have a 401(k) plan in which you may choose to participate. For others, there is a mandatory minimum participation that your company requires. It is usually a small amount like 1-2% or so.

If your company does not offer a 401(k) option you may participate in one of your own choosing by setting up a 401(k) through a

Bank, Credit Union, or a private investment firm. Consider starting to pay yourself immediately for if you don't provide for yourself, who will? For self employed individuals who work alone or who have a small business and choose not to have a 401(k) program in place, this privately funded method is the only choice available.

The great advantage about entering into a 401(k) plan at work is that many employers participate in a dollar matching feature for funds you contribute. Most will match what you contribute up to a ceiling of 5-10%. Here are four things for your consideration: 1. Many companies may allow you to contribute more than 5-10% of your income. Check with your HR director for company policies. 2. The law permits contributions of up to $15,500 per year if under 50 years of age, or $20,500 per person per year if over 50 years of age. Check with your tax advisor. 3. Your company may have a dollar matching feature. It varies from one company to another…it may be 50 cents on the dollar or it may be a 100% match of dollar for dollar or even more. However, in most companies the match usually declines in percentage as you contribute more of your income. 4. In essence, by matching your contributions, your company is offering to give you free money. Your employer's contributions may add up to approximately two to four weeks of salary per year. Check it out and then take advantage of this program. After all, it is "free money," that when compounded over a long period of time may equal many thousands of dollars.

One of the greatest benefits of the company matching 401(k) plan is that your contributions are made from pre tax dollars. This has the effect of lowering your present taxable income, and allows you to defer your tax obligations on your 401K until your retirement. At that time you will almost certainly be in a lower tax bracket than you are at the time the monies were contributed.

Employers usually offer investment choices that may be limited to a few investment options. These are chosen with the needs of your entire company or work force in mind, and while you may desire other choices you would miss the matching funds feature should you go elsewhere. You may elect to contribute at work in order to get the free match and then start a personal account outside your work environment. Do your research, make your decision, and begin participating in the plan of your choosing, either employer plans, private plans, or both.

The key is that you are paying yourself first and you are investing in your future. If you don't do it for yourself, nobody will do it for you.

Roth IRAs

Roth IRAs are unique and are another highly favorable option. A Roth IRA is unique because it allows you to invest with after-tax dollars. Since you have paid the tax on the front end of the investment your money is non-taxable when it is withdrawn. Even the interest is non-taxable. The present limit is $5000 per person per year, or $6,000 per year if you are over age 50. Everyone should strongly consider starting a new fully-funded Roth IRA each year. An investor is able to start a new Roth each year before the following April 15 deadline. They are as easy to set up as a traditional IRA, you just have to set it up as a Roth and contribute after-tax dollars. Talk to your investment advisor to learn more about Roth IRAs.

Certificates of Deposit

Better known as CDs, these are savings instruments offered by banks and credit unions to encourage you to save money. CDs are also tools used by banks to enable you to lend them your money. They receive your money in the form of a CD and they use it to make more money for themselves. CDs are among the safest possible investments you can make because in most cases they are guaranteed (currently up to $250,000 per depositor per bank,) by the Federal Government's FDIC program; the Federal Deposit Insurance Corporation. Presently, they are not a very good option for someone who wants to build wealth for retirement. The reason they are not good investment opportunities is the fact that they are safe places to PARK money. CDs are not designed to make your money appreciate in value in today's economy. They earn interest within the range of less than one percent up to a high of approximately five percent. At best, CDs only keep abreast with the rate of inflation. However, they are a great place to park money when you may need access to it in a hurry. For example, you sell your house and are handed a cashier's check at closing. You plan to buy another house within a few months so you deposit the money in a short term CD. That makes sense because it draws interest and it is readily available when you need it. CD terms of deposit range from 7 days, 30 days, 90 days, 180 days, 1 year, and longer. You select how long the term of deposit will be and deposit your money accordingly. WARNING: should you need your money and withdraw it before the CD matures, you will incur a financial penalty. Check with your banker and understand the full terms of the contract before depositing your money in a CD. This way you will have no surprises.

Bonds

There are many types of bonds available for investors. Among the best investments are municipal tax-free bonds offered by certain cities. Utilities and other public entities also offer bonds for sale, some of which are tax-free. Bonds are generally a very safe investment instrument and can help you build some wealth without a lot of risk. Talk with your trusted financial advisor or broker to gain a better understanding of bonds and how you can include them in your portfolio.

Diversify Your Assets

A friend of mine lost his retirement savings of $640,000 because he had invested the entire amount in one company…Enron. He did not diversify. Diversifying your investments simply means that you have your monies spread out over many different accounts. If one or two fail, you still have the rest. If one or more loses money you may still make money in the other six.

The Bible talks about the concept of investing and diversity in the book of Ecclesiastes 11:1-3. "Cast your bread upon the waters, for after many days you will find it again. Give portions to seven, yes to eight, for you do not know what disaster may come upon the land. If clouds are full of water, they pour rain upon the earth. Whether a tree falls to the south or to the north, in the place where it falls, there will it lie." Verse one encourages a person to invest their money to cause it to grow. Verse two emphasizes diversity saying that invested money should be divided into seven or eight different accounts because one does not know what could happen to bring about a loss. Verse three states matter-of-factly that when trouble comes, it comes, does its damage, and so be it.

PRINCIPLE: GOOD STEWARDSHIP INCLUDES INVESTING MONEY DIVERSELY

The Bible encourages you to invest. It also encourages you to diversify. That is both awesome and sophisticated advice. Do some further study of your own in Ecclesiastes 11 verses 4-10 and you will find that they reveal other principles which say that the person who fears risk does not invest and will not see their money grow; that the mighty works of God cannot be fully understood; that we should invest with diversity because we can't possibly know which accounts will do well and which will not. These verses also suggest that a person who invests and loses money will remember his losses, that you should rejoice in your youth and remove sorrow from your heart.

Jesus highlighted aspects of the concept of investing when he spoke of the talents in Matthew 25:14-29. Here, three servants were given various amounts of money to invest for their master and earn more while he was away on business. Two of the three were successful in their ventures, while the third was afraid and hid his master's money in the ground. The two successful servants were commended and rewarded, while the unsuccessful servant had his talent stripped from him and he was reprimanded for not investing his master's money.

WITHDRAWING YOUR FUNDS AT RETIREMENT

When it is time for you to retire you will be responsible for notifying your retirement account custodians of your change in status. Depending upon your retirement plan, you will have various options. You may wish to receive your money immediately, or you may wish to continue contributing to your account and allowing it to grow for a few more years. There are various ways to receive money from your retirement accounts. Check with qualified people and seek sound advice before signing or doing anything. If you are retiring from a business or a company, your HR representative is there to help you with this process. In addition to talking with your HR resource, you may wish to contact your local Social Security office approximately six months in advance of your planned retirement date. Someone there can provide the information you need and guide you through their process.

WHAT HAPPENS TO MY 401(K) OR IRA IF I CHANGE JOBS?

Following are some general facts covering rollovers. Check with your HR person or financial advisor for sound advice before making any decision or before doing or signing anything. This section simply highlights some of the options that are available, and it is not the intention of this author to make any financial recommendations. You may wish to make those decisions with the guidance of a financial advisor. Consider the following.

1. You can leave it with your former company. (Check with your HR department to see if you meet your company's vesting requirements that would allow you to keep your company's portion of the matching funds as part of your retirement. Most companies have a modest time requirement so most readers will be fine. But, check to make sure if you are contemplating a career move.)

2. You can roll it over to your new company's 401(k) or IRA plan if they have one and you like it. (This is very common and is called a "trustee to trustee" transfer.)

3. You can roll it over to a private plan if it suits you best.

4. You can cash it out. (If your account is valued at $5,000.00 or less, your employer may insist that you cash it out of their plan or do a "trustee to trustee" transfer.)

URGENT WARNING: At the time of this writing, the Federal Government allows only 60 days to roll funds over into another 401(k) or IRA should you cash them out or withdraw them from your company without a "trustee to trustee" transfer. If you don't roll them over before the 60 day period expires, the IRS will be knocking on your door asking for their portion of your retirement account…the taxes you owe, and you would likely incur the 10% penalty of the total amount as well.

One other category needs to be addressed: "Highly Compensated" employees may not be allowed to contribute as high a percentage of their salary as some of the lower paid employees. At the time of this writing the "Highly Compensated" employee threshold starts at the $105,000 per year income level.

WHAT DO I DO WHEN I REACH RETIREMENT AGE?

Following are some general facts covering distributions. Check with your HR person or financial advisor for sound advice before making any decision or before doing or signing anything. When your longed-for day of retirement arrives you may have one major question that deserves an answer: "How do I access my 401(k) or IRA?" You will have several options to consider. You will want to talk with a qualified advisor before making your choice in order to give yourself the greatest advantage possible. At the time of this writing, the following options were available:

1. A lump sum distribution whereby you may withdraw all your monies in one lump sum at one time.

2. Leave your money where it is in order that it may continue growing. You are allowed to leave it there totally untouched until you reach age 70 ½, at which time the IRS requires you to take mandatory annual distributions.

3. Roll your funds into another retirement plan like an IRA unless you have reached your 70 ½ age requirement. (Note that the 401(k) has some advantages the IRA doesn't have such as protection from your creditors should you have to pursue bankruptcy or should you be involved in a lawsuit, and your 401(k) is almost always less expensive to maintain if left with your company until age 70 ½ due to IRA maintenance fees. Yet, if you are in a low performing 401(k), you may offset the higher fees by higher earnings in the IRA. Get appropriate reliable advice before you make any major decisions.)

4. An annuity may be set up to guarantee you a fixed income for the rest of your life. Your spouse may be designated to receive a fixed amount after your death. An annuity is the one viable option if your desire is to have a guaranteed income for life. There are some disadvantages. They include the fact that you may die sooner than you expected, and you will not have had access to all your money at one time. But that is balanced by the fact that you and your spouse will receive a monthly check as long as either of you lives.

SOCIAL SECURITY

Social Security benefits have been a godsend for the majority of its recipients. However, you may be in for a surprise at some point in your future because as it now exists, Social Security is unsustainable. Look for some radical changes in the coming years, because if Congress leaves Social Security unchanged, it will cease to exist sometime in the 2030s. Experts say that it will come to an end because much more will be needed in funding than can be generated by workers paying into the program. The Year 2030 sounds so far in the future. It may be distant, but if you aren't prepared for Social Security's eventual demise, you will pay the price with your retirement when you are ready to draw your first check only to find that it isn't there.

One of the best things you can do for yourself and your family is to make your own arrangements for your future retirement funds exclusive of Social Security. If you provide your own funds, and Social Security exists when you retire, it will be a retirement windfall you hadn't planned on receiving.

Our nation's financial landscape would have looked totally different than it does today, had our churches, schools, universities, and our federal government begun teaching the Pay Yourself First principle at the end of World War II. Had FDR proposed this radical approach to retirement in the 1930s instead of creating the Social Security Administration, we would not have needed a federally mandated retirement program.

That is enough "What if" thinking. One of the most important financial steps you can ever take is that of paying yourself first. If you will discipline yourself and learn to manage your finances by the 10/90 Principle you will be investing in both yours and your family's future. Look at what following the 10/90 Principle could do for you.

10/90 Principle Produces Results

In order to see the power of paying yourself first and avoiding a skimpy retirement, consider this hypothetical situation. Aaron and Andy each started investing $200 per month in ROTH IRAs. Neither one of them ever missed a month of investing. They both earned 12% on their investments each year. Aaron started at age 30 and Andy started at age 40. They retire on the same day at age 65. Aaron's contributions the first year totaled $2,536.50, while Andy's were $0. By the end of the tenth year, Aaron's investment totaled $46,007.74, while Andy's were $0. By the end of year 11, Aaron's investment totaled $54,379.17, while Andy contributed his first $2,536.50. By the end of year 15, Aaron's investment totaled $99,916.04, while Andy's totaled $16,333.93. Fast forward…by the end of year 30, Aaron's investment totaled $698,922.83, while Andy's totaled $197.851.07. The day that they both retired at age 65, Aaron and Andy had each contributed $2,536.50 per year. Both contributed that same amount each and every year. However, Aaron contributed that amount for 35 years, while Andy contributed that amount for 25 years. Each man had done well. Aaron's account totaled $1,286,191.89, while Andy's account totaled $375,769.33.

TIME EQUALS A LOT MORE MONEY

- Aaron and Andy both retire on the same day at age 65.

- Aaron's retirement account is worth $1,286,191.89

- Andy' retirement account is worth $ 375,769.33

Both made exactly the same $200 per month investment into identical ROTH IRA accounts that increased 12% each year. By starting 10 years earlier than Andy, Aaron' account was worth $910,422.56 more than Andy's. Ten years equaled almost $1 million dollars difference.

CONSIDER FOLLOWING THE 10/90 PRINCIPLE BY PAYING YOURSELF FIRST!

Chapter 13
Taming the "Lone Ranger" Monster

A long time ago I came to the conclusion that there were a lot of people who were much smarter than me and that they would be willing to offer counsel if asked. Ladies, what is one of the toughest things for a guy to do when he gets lost while driving a car? Right! It is really tough for him to stop and ask someone for directions. Most guys will drive for miles and miles when the simplest thing would have been to stop and ask someone for directions. Guys, do we feel that we are superior, infallible, and incapable of making a mistake, have an attitude, or what? Many wives just answered: "All of the above!" One of the toughest things for many men to admit is that they are wrong.

Many men, and women alike, are stuck in a "Lone Ranger" mode when it comes to making decisions or doing almost anything else in life. One of the toughest monsters to defeat is that of feeling, acting, and living as though you needed no one else on the planet. However, this monster can be defeated by a simple process. We will get to that in a minute but first, have you ever noticed that many Christians, churches, and Christian organizations make the following mistake when planning. First, they work hard and make their wonderful, exciting, admirable, and ambitious plans. Second, they stop and ask the Lord to bless their completed plans. What is wrong with this picture? Note the following four problems with this process. 1. The plan is THEIR plan… God was not involved in it at all. It is their plan. 2. They INVITE God to bless something that may be totally out of his will. 3. They EXPECT God to bless something that may be outside his will, and God refuses to do that. 4. They WONDER why their plan is not working…it is obvious, God is not in it.

A great strategy for breaking out of the "Lone Ranger" mold is to invite others into your personal world. If you decided that you were going to build your dream house, what is the first and most important thing you would need? Other people. Unless you were a master carpenter who could complete the project singlehandedly, you would need other people to help you build your house. If you are in the process of making a life-changing decision what is the first thing you need? You need input from God and honest input from other trusted friends who will listen to you and give you honest feedback. If you seek it, God will reveal his will to you. Your friends can be a sounding-board for your ideas, dreams, fears, and the decisions you are facing. You and I were created with the need for other people. When God created Adam the very next thing he did was to create Eve. There are many ways one can break out of the "Lone Ranger" mold, but taking the two steps outlined below would be an excellent starting point for anyone who wishes to involve others in their life.

1. INVOLVE JESUS

Try to imagine the wording a Christian would use in a prayer asking the Lord to bless the plans he made without God's input. We don't know the exact words one might pray, but whatever those words might be, I wonder if they might sound something like this when they reach the ears of the Lord: *"Lord, please bless this mess."*

God loves planning. He devised the greatest plan of all time when he created His plan of Salvation. God loves to be included in our plans and wants to be involved in them from the very beginning. He loves to bless our plans. He especially loves blessing our plans that have included him in our planning process from the very beginning.

Ask the Lord to guide you as you construct your plans, not after your plan is already made. Read what God says in the New Testament book of James 4:13-17. "Now listen, you who say, 'Today or tomorrow we will go to this or that city, spend a year there, carry on business and make money.' Why, you do not even know what will happen tomorrow. What is your life? You are a mist that appears for a little while and then vanishes. Instead, you ought to say, 'If it is the Lord's will, we will live and do this or that.' As it is, you boast and brag. All such boasting is evil. Anyone, then, who knows the good he ought to do and doesn't do it, sins."

Involve God in your planning process. He offers counsel, sound judgment, understanding, and power. Another appropriate verse is Proverbs 8:14: "Counsel and sound judgment are mine; I have understanding and power." When planning something, just think how much better off you would be to have God at your side helping you make your plans. God offers counsel, sound judgment, understanding, and power.

Don't make the mistake of making your plans first, and then coming back and asking the Lord to bless them. My elderly grandmother "Memo" used to say: "Don't put the cart before the horse." The horse-drawn cart only works when the horse is hitched to the front. Putting the cart in front of the horse guarantees that the horse can't pull the cart, and he sure can't push it. The end result would be a totally useless folly…a horse and a cart neither of which can do what they are designed to do. Planning first and then asking God to bless our plans is a totally ridiculous situation.

If you make your plans without the Lord's involvement, you have gone about the process backwards. How do you ask God to help you plan? First, in prayer you ask the Lord to guide you in making your plans. How do you follow God's leadership in the planning process? You begin to make your plans with his input. You do this by praying about every aspect of your plan, and you listen for the Holy Spirit's leadership. As you begin to plan with God's help, you may discover that he will bless some of your plans without you even having to ask him. Is it permissible to ask God to bless my plans? Sure it is OK for you to ask him to bless them. He just wants to help you make plans that are best for you and your family and that will honor him. How may I know whether my plans honor God? Ask and answer the following questions about each and every plan you make. Does this plan go along with or against God's Word? Is any aspect of this plan sinful, harmful to anyone? Will this plan it bring glory to God, or will it bring shame or disrespect upon the name of Jesus in any way? Add questions of your own.

Consider the following verses from the Psalms that describe how God can bless you with his wisdom and counsel.
- "I will praise the Lord, who counsels me; even at night my heart instructs me" Psalm 16:7.
- "I will instruct you and teach you in the way you should go; I will counsel you and watch over you" Psalm 32:8.
- "You guide me with your counsel, and afterward you will take me into glory" Psalm 73:24.
- "Your statutes are my delight; they are my counselors" Psalm 119:24.

2. INVOLVE OTHERS

I started this chapter by saying that a long time ago I came to the conclusion that there were a lot of people who were smarter than me and that they would be willing to offer valuable counsel if asked. In your journey toward showing your money who's boss, be sure and involve your spouse, your family, a trusted friend, godly people, or someone who can offer sound advice and good counsel. Several verses in the book of Proverbs talk about seeking guidance, wisdom, and counsel from God and other people.
- "For lack of guidance a nation falls, but many advisers make victory sure" Proverbs 11:14.
- "Plans fail for lack of counsel, but with many advisers they succeed" Proverbs 15:22.
- "Counsel and sound judgment are mine; I have understanding and power" Proverbs 8:14.

Bill thought that involving someone else in planning showed personal weakness. He had been taught to be self-sufficient and that real macho men didn't need anybody's help. Just the opposite is true. You show great strength and wisdom by involving God and someone who has either been there before or who has had that same experience you are now facing. If they have been there, gained wisdom or knowledge, have learned from their experience, and can pass some wisdom and knowledge along to you, you may benefit greatly from them. When you go to someone for counsel you are not asking them to make your plans for you. You are asking them for wisdom, knowledge, advice, and perspective. If you are wise, you will seek out all the wisdom, advice, and perspective you can get from trustworthy people.

NOT ALL ADVICE IS GOOD ADVICE

Finally, just because someone gives you advice doesn't mean you have to accept it. Not all advice is valuable advice. Not all wisdom is godly wisdom. Not all perspective is the proper perspective. You must be wise enough to know the good from the bad and you must be mature enough to apply only the good and reject the faulty advice.

GOD CARES ABOUT YOUR FUTURE

God loves and accepts you just as you are right now. He knows all about your past successes and failures. He knows every single sin you have ever committed. He knows about each and every mistake you have ever made. The wonderful truth is that he loves and accepts you anyway in spite of all of them. God's unconditional acceptance of you is his awesome unconditional love in action. It is all about his wonderful grace. No matter where you have been in your life or where you are right now, God wants to help you and bless you beyond your wildest dreams. God is far more concerned with where you go from this point in your life than he is with where you have been. Accept God's grace and unconditional love. Appropriate it for your very own. Tell him about your failures. Confess your past sins. Repent, or turn away from them. Accept Christ Jesus as your Savior and Lord. Make him the controlling partner of your life. Do all these things and watch out for the wonderful things that he will do in your life and in your family's life as well.

"What about my past," you ask. "Is God is concerned about my past and where I have been and what I have done? Is he concerned with the mistakes I have made and the sins I have committed? Is he concerned about my bad decisions and poor planning?" Yes, he is concerned. But his concern may be for a different reason than you think. His concerns center on the consequences of those sins, mistakes, and decisions. He is concerned about how they have impacted your life and the lives of others. Sins impact us and others in negative, destructive, and hurtful ways. God is concerned about our past because of the destruction it can have both upon us and other people. God doesn't want your past to keep hurting you and other people. God's concern reflects his awesome unconditional love. If he didn't love you, he wouldn't care.

There is hope. You can ask for and receive God's forgiveness. With his help you can put those sins and all your negative past behind you. You can begin a new life that will both serve and honor Jesus. You have a responsibility to God and others. You have a responsibility to ask others for forgiveness and to make restitution. You have a responsibility to right the wrongs and ease the pains you have inflicted upon other people. You can learn from your past sins, mistakes, and bad decisions and commit to not repeating those sins and destructive actions again and again.

You can become a disciple of the Lord Jesus Christ. "A disciple, I thought Jesus only had twelve of them, and they are all dead now," you say. Right, his original twelve disciples are dead. Today, every born-again Christian can become a disciple. The word disciple has a simple meaning: "learner." To be a "learner," qualifies you to become a disciple. You become a disciple when you become a serious and devoted follower of Jesus Christ. Discipleship is not an "in name only" title or position. It is the real deal. Jesus wants to have you to join his team. Many of you have already joined his team and are actively following the Lord. Others can join right now by asking Jesus to be your Savior and by asking him to forgive all your sins, and then become a deeply committed follower or disciple of his.

The following verses talk about counting the cost of discipleship. "Suppose one of you wants to build a tower. Will he not first sit down and estimate the cost to see if he has enough money to complete it? For if he lays the foundation and is not able to finish it, everyone who sees it will ridicule him, saying, 'This fellow began to build and was not able to finish'" Luke 14:28-30.

Commit yourself to Jesus. Start involving him in all your plans and watch your plans be blessed with God's success. The secondary meaning of the verses above offers good advice about planning. Don't start a building project unless you have the money to finish it. That principle of counting the cost can be applied to every plan anyone can possibly conceive. Consider putting it into practice within your own life. You, your family, and your business will be the winners. Jesus was a planner and he had valuable things to say about planning.

A Lesson About Forgiveness

So you have made some mistakes along the way by not planning, by making bad decisions, or by simply making some mistakes in life. Welcome to the human race. We have all made mistakes and bad decisions. Allow God to pick you up, dust you off, and get you started back on the road to life. Tell God about your sins and mistakes. Ask for his forgiveness, and then get on with the rest of your life. A wise father decided to teach his son a lesson about forgiveness and the consequences of lying to his parents. He had his son drive three large nails into a beautifully finished oak board. Once he finished hammering the nails, the father explained that the nails represented the sins the young man had recently committed.

He explained that since he had confessed the sins and had asked for both God's and his father's forgiveness he had received it. Next he asked his son to take the hammer and remove the three nails to symbolize his newfound forgiveness. Though he struggled, he finally was able to pull them out. His father then said: "Just as the nails have been removed from the board, God, your mother, and I have forgiven you." He pointed to the three holes where the nails had been and wiped a tear from his eye. Then he said: "Son, the consequences of your sins remain. The holes will never go away. Let them always remind you that your sins will leave their marks in your own life and within the lives of others." His father embraced him and said: "Son, every time we sin, we leave consequences behind."

Remember, Christians aren't perfect, just forgiven. All have made and will continue to make some bad decisions. Thank God for his grace and forgiveness. All of our decisions have consequences. This wisdom applies to decisions of every type. Financial, spiritual, family, career, education, retirement, and every other decision you could ever make. The key is to always make the best decisions you possibly can make, and deal with the negative consequences of your bad decisions in the best ways possible…turn them over to God. Take your financial situation as it exists today and make the most of it. You can gain control of your money by showing your money who's boss. You can gain control of your "Lone Ranger" mentality by humbling yourself before God, your family, and your coworkers by seeking godly advice and input.

Chapter 14
Taming the Decision-Making Monster

Aron Ralston displayed the personal courage of a true American hero. Aron was an experienced mountaineer who was hiking in the Canyonlands National Park south of Moab, Utah in the spring of 2003. He called upon himself to do the unthinkable, the impossible; because of his decisive actions he saved his own life. His crisis began when he became trapped in a narrow space in the rocks with his arm pinned under a gigantic boulder. He remained in this predicament for days, ran out of water, and came to the stark realization that unless he took charge of the situation he would die there all alone. In order to survive, Ralston took his pocket knife and amputated his own arm just below the elbow. He administered first aid, and rappelled off the rock face to the ground below where he hiked out of the mountains to rescuers who had been searching for him. Given the same set of circumstances lesser people would have died. Aron Ralston is a hero in everyone's estimation.

Uncertainty is best handled when faced with decisiveness. Decisiveness is most effective when tempered with good decision making skills. Being decisive is one thing. Being decisive and right is an entirely different scenario. Countless people have been decisive in situations that demanded immediate actions. However wonderful it is during times of crisis, decisiveness alone is not enough. The most beneficial result is to have the ability to make the right decision while being decisive at the same time.

Miracle on the Hudson River

One of the greatest acts of heroism ever witnessed took place in January 2009 when US Airways flight 1549 Captain Chesley B. "Sulley"

Sullenberger, and Copilot Jeffrey Skiles, landed their Airbus A310 in the middle of the Hudson River just off Manhattan. Bound from New York's LaGuardia Airport to Charlotte, NC, the flight carried a total of 155 people on board. The captain reported that he experienced a double bird strike within a minute after takeoff. With 1000% certainty, Sullenberger and Skiles made the right decision. They were decisive and they were right. Those rare qualities, when coupled together, are capable of producing amazing results. Had they not been decisive and had they not made the right decision, there is a high probability that many of the passengers and crew would not be alive today. Many refer to this heroic act as the "Miracle on the Hudson." A miracle no doubt, as passengers reported that everyone on the plane was praying as they awaited impact. We salute the three flight attendants: Shelia Dail, Donna Dent, Doreen Welsh, and passengers who assisted with the evacuation of the stricken plane. No one will ever forget the pictures of the passengers standing upon the wings awaiting rescue from the brave men and women who came to their aid. Great job all of you! God is so good!

A friend of mine once said: "We don't know what we would do in a crisis situation unless we are actually in that situation." He was right, and spoke from his own personal experience. He had just recently passed one of life's ultimate tests by saving a man's life that was facing certain death. As he described his experience he said that something deep within motivated him to spring into action and caused him to refuse to panic.

PRINCIPLE: EXTRAORDINARY TIMES DEMAND EXTRAORDINARY RESPONSES

At the heart of this principle is the fact that you can't just keep doing the same things you have always done in every situation in life. There are extraordinary times when extraordinary responses are needed. There are times when something deep within you has to kick in and be followed. It's the kind of stuff that heroes are made of. Heroes are made during extraordinary moments of intense tragedy when someone steps forward to take charge of the situation. They quickly do the right thing, and they bring about the best possible ending. That "something" which happens is what we are talking about. It is an elusive intangible called good decision-making ability. You can learn to make good decisions.

During extraordinary times, being right can reward you while being wrong can cost you. Remember my mentioning of my Enron investor friend? He was forced to watch his doomed Enron stock plummet along with his life savings of $640,000. After the legal wrangling of a class-action lawsuit, he had a final settlement of about $3,000. He had lost more than 99.5% of his investment. Had he sold his stock one month prior to the freefall he would have been fine. But once the fall started, his Enron shares couldn't be sold so he watched in horror as his retirement nest egg evaporated right before his eyes.

Americans are living in the toughest economic times since the Great Depression of the 1930s. Not many have experienced an economic meltdown quite like this. Millions of people have either lost their homes, their jobs, their cars, their 401(k) nest eggs, their boats, their furs, their motorcycles, their jewelry, and a thousand other assets.

Others have lost faith in our economic system, our political system, hope for a stable economic future, and their sense of dignity or self worth. Some lost their families due to the severe financial distresses that overwhelmed them.

PRINCIPLE: TO SHOW YOUR MONEY WHO'S BOSS, FOCUS ON YOUR FUTURE

To show your money who's boss and tame the money monsters that rear their ugly heads in your financial life, you will need to focus on the future. Along with most of the humans on the planet, you and I have made our share of stupid financial decisions. We have wasted money, lost money, and thrown money away. We have spent money we should not have spent, spent money we didn't have, spent our house or car payments, and made a number of other ridiculous spending decisions. No matter where you have been in your financial past, what matters now are your present and your future. Admittedly, past decisions concerning your career, housing, education, debts, savings, investing, and discretionary spending will have repercussions. Some of the repercussions were good and some were bad. Some of those repercussions will have results that will extend beyond the present into the future. For instance, did you unwittingly stumble into a sub-prime mortgage? Did you over allocate your retirement funds by putting everything in aggressive growth stocks? Did you over-spend on your last vehicle purchase? These and other decisions weren't your best decisions. Did you ever lament: "If only I had known then what I know now?" Don't beat up on yourself. You have already taken a pretty tough beating because of the economy, so don't pile on. Now, let's get back to showing your money who's boss. Living in the past accomplishes nothing. Living in the future accomplishes nothing. The key to living is to live in the present while learning from our past and keeping an eye on the future. Now, let's move on to consider 10 tangible things you can do to better yourself, your family, and your financial future. These 10 things can help you gain a head start on reaching your goal of showing your money that you are boss. Remember, Christians aren't perfect, just forgiven.

10 Steps to Personal Transformation

1. Celebrate Your Good Decisions

Celebrate the fact that some of your financial decisions were, and are, fantastic. You had a decision to make, you prayed about it, did your research, made your decision, and it worked out just like you hoped it would. Congratulate yourself, your spouse, your kids, and pat yourself on the back. Go out to a nice restaurant and have dinner. Have your best friends over for a great evening of food and fellowship. Send flowers to your wife. Cook your husband's favorite meal. Make up a "World's Greatest Mom," or "World's Greatest Dad," tee shirt and let the kids present it to her or him. Openly brag about your spouse and his or her great decision in front of your kids.

Everyone loves a compliment. You can change your families' entire outlook on life by practicing the following. Never let a single day go by without complimenting your spouse and each of your children for something good they did that day. Aside from the fact that they might wonder whether you sustained a bump to your head, you will do wonders for their confidence and self-esteem. Start a revolution in your home by genuinely complimenting everyone living there at least once a day for something good they have done. Lead your family in a prayer of thanksgiving to the Lord for his great blessings. Acknowledge him for giving you the opportunity and the insight that you used in making the decision(s) that led to your successful results.

2. Learn from Your Bad Decisions

You blew it. You made a bad spending decision. You should have made a different decision but you didn't. Instead of making a good decision, you made a bad one. Relax and set yourself at ease. You don't have to try to be perfect all the time. There was only one perfect man who ever lived and they crucified him. Be a big enough man to admit to God, your family, and your friends that you made some mistakes. This may be tough. "Me, admit that I was wrong? Why, you're crazy. Admitting that I was wrong and made some mistakes is nothing but showing my weakness. I'm not weak, I'm strong." No, you are not strong, you are bull-headed. You are stubborn. Everybody on this planet makes mistakes…everybody but you, right? No, you make them too; you are just not man enough to admit it. You are weak. You are a guy with an overly inflated ego. You are acting foolishly by trying to cover up your weaknesses and failures by appearing to be strong. Hey, want to show some real strength? Want to be a man's man? You can show real strength by admitting that you are not God, that you do make some mistakes, that you do sometimes fail, and that you are not infallible.

The Apostle Paul, a man's man, said it like this: "Therefore I take pleasure in infirmities, in reproaches, in necessities, in persecutions, in distresses for Christ's sake: for when I am weak, then am I strong" 2 Corinthians 12:10.

In baseball, any player who is able to hit the ball and advance to first base three out of ten times is considered a star. If someone can get on base four out of ten tries he would be considered to be a superstar. Let this fact sink in for a minute. A guy who fails seven out of ten times…and he is still a star baseball player? Yes. He is a star. Do you get it? You don't have to bat 1000 either in baseball or in life to be a success. You don't have to have a track record that is 100% perfect to be successful. Do you remember how many times Thomas Edison failed to discover the right filament before he invented the light bulb? This is not an exaggeration, but it took Edison more than 1,000 attempts before he found the right answer. At best, that is a ratio of 1,000: 1. That equals failure in anybody's book. Anybody's book except Edison's that is. What if he had stopped experimenting after 500 tries?

3. Accept the Fact that You are Human

So you have made some bad decisions. You may have lost your house, your job, or your 401(k). That doesn't mean that you are a bad person. It doesn't mean that you are a failure. It does mean that you are a human like all the rest of us and you made some bad decisions along the way. That's all it means. Welcome to the human race. What you choose to do now is what really matters. Will you be satisfied to simply sit and sulk, meditate and mope, review and rebuke, dog yourself and get depressed? Or will you get up and get on with the remainder of your life like the Old Testament King David? David didn't just make a bad spending decision; he committed adultery, had the woman's husband killed, took the woman for his own wife, and tried to cover the whole thing up. He sinned. He made several horrible mistakes, experienced a terrible moral failure in his personal life but, he repented, prayed to the Lord for forgiveness, and received it. After receiving God's forgiveness he got up, took a bath, put on some clean clothes, and got on with the rest of his life. Later he wrote Psalm 51 to reflect his experience of confession of his sins, his contrition and God's forgiveness. Hey, it's up to you. Reach down deep within and put your faith in God and get up and get going. Do what King David did. Pray to the Lord, confess every sin you can possibly remember, tell the Lord you are sorry, repent from those sins, ask God to forgive you, and tell him that you want him to change your life and to give you a fresh start. Accept his forgiveness and celebrate by getting on with the rest of your life.

4. Put Your Past Behind

Forget the past. You can't change the bad financial or spending decisions you made in the past. They are over. Deliberately move into the present and have fun living once again. Too many people spend most of their lives ruminating over what went wrong, where they failed, and why they should be miserable. All of this is coming from the past. Get with it. Put all that old baggage behind you. The only things you need to keep from the past are your past memories. Remember the good things and the bad. Remember the bad things so that you can learn from your mistakes and not make them again. Part of learning to make good decisions is the practice of learning to think things through before you make a decision. Prayerfully include God and his will in your decision making. As you are getting ready to make a decision, examine all your options and choose the best one. Develop a financial survival plan and live in the present.

One guy who probably made many more disastrous mistakes in his early life than any person one could name had this to say about his past: "Not that I…have already been made perfect, but I press on to take hold of that for which Christ Jesus took hold of me…But one thing I do: Forgetting what is behind and straining toward what is ahead, I press on toward the goal to win the prize for which God has called me heavenward in Christ Jesus" Philippians 3:12-13.

Paul chose to put the negative things of his past behind him. Paul had relegated his past to the past. You can choose to do like Paul and put your past behind you. Some of the key verses in the Word of God which will help you deal with your past are found in Psalm 103: "…Praise the LORD, O my soul, and forget not all his benefits, who forgives all your sins and heals all your diseases, who redeems your life from the pit and crowns you with love and compassion, who satisfies your desires with good things so that your youth is renewed like the eagle's…he does not treat us as our sins deserve or repay us according to our iniquities. For as high as the heavens are above the earth, so great is his love for those who fear him; as far as the east is from the west, so far has he removed our transgressions from us. As a father has compassion on his children, so the LORD has compassion on those who fear him; for he knows how we are formed, he remembers that we are dust."

You can put your past and your past sins and mistakes behind by:
- learning to praise the Lord
- remembering all he has done for you
- confessing your sins and accepting his forgiveness
- receiving his blessings, being renewed, and abiding in his love

- realizing that he has separated you from the sins you confessed as far as the east is from the west
- by accepting his loving compassion toward you as a kind Heavenly Father.

Paul knew how to deal with failure. He knew that earlier in his life he had failed miserably by being a legalist and by persecuting Christians by subjecting them to beatings and jail. He also knew how to celebrate his successes. He deliberately chose to put his past behind him and strive with all his might toward the goal to win the prize that lay ahead of him. The prize was serving Jesus and going to heaven one day.

Can you imagine anyone carrying a 60 pound backpack on their back for the rest of their life without ever removing it? That is what you are doing if you carry all your past junk around with you. You know...all your emotional junk from your past failures. Take the pack off, lay it down, get with the plan, and live in the present.

Apply this principle to your life...deal with your past failures and sins by confessing them to the Lord. Repent – turn away from them, put them behind you, and press ahead toward the future with a new attitude and a proper perspective. Living in the past and wallowing in your past failures and mistakes offers absolutely nothing except misery. What if you did lose your life savings? What if you did lose your house? What if you did lose your job? You now have a gift that can be seen as either a curse or a blessing. You may choose to see it as a blessing in that you get to start over and do things differently this time. Neither Paul nor Thomas Edison let failures stop them. They both kept charging ahead. You can do the same thing. Everyone has heard the expression: "fall forward." You may wish to apply it like this: "FAIL FORWARD." Be one of the few persons out of 100 people who will examine his failures and allow them to thrust him ahead instead of allowing them to hold him back.

5. LEARN TO ACCEPT SUCCESS

One of the most difficult things for some people to learn is to learn to accept success. All forms of success, not just financial success. This inability seems to go back to the fact that some people feel that they are unworthy of good things, including success. God loves it when you succeed in ways that glorify him. He is your biggest fan. You can reprogram your thinking to know that God rejoices when you succeed and that he wants you to be able to rejoice in your successes also. God wants you to have lots of successes in your life. Learn to see you successes as blessings from God.

6. ATTITUDE ADJUSTMENT

There is truth in the cliché: "Your Attitude determines your Altitude." Now would be a great time for you to check your attitude and pattern it after the Scripture the Lord gave us through Paul. Everyone has an attitude or outlook with which they approach life. What is yours? Is it anything like the outlook described by one of the following words?

Victorious	God is in control: together we can handle anything
Positive	I'm positive that God will make everything work out best
Good	Optimistic, Confident, Hopeful
Neutral	It may work out or it may not
Negative	Defeated, Lost Hope
Victim	Poor me. I don't deserve this. Who did this to me?

You can choose to adopt any one of these attitudes or outlooks any time you want. You probably already vacillate between two or three of them at different times during your week. We choose the attitude or outlook we have. We get to choose what type of person we become. We choose how we relate to God, our families, our fellow employees or fellow business partners and so on. Sure, we are born with a certain set of skills, including our natural God-given abilities, talents, personality traits, and the way we relate to people. These might be likened to our default settings. But default settings can be changed. Some things have been governed by your circumstances; such as the kind of parents you had, the family in which you grew up, the teachers you had, the schools you attended, and the jobs you have held. This overall experience becomes the summary or grand total of your life to this point. But those are the key words of this thought…TO THIS POINT.

You can choose to take charge of the rest of your life and with the Lord's help, adopt a different approach to the way you handle things. This is one of the problems. We allow circumstances, events, people, and emotions to govern our feelings and to dictate our attitudes and outlooks. This is normal because we are humans. Only machines are unaffected by most external circumstances. For example, your PC doesn't really know, or really care whether you are having a bad day. It can't tell what kind of mood you are in or tell whether you made great or lousy decisions with your finances. It, like your car, is just a machine.

7. Renew Your Mind

Decide what kind of attitude / outlook you want to have in life. Do your best to begin positioning yourself to experiencing that outlook most of the time. With a lot of prayer, Bible study, patience, and practice you will one day wake up and see that you now maintain that attitude most of the time. God's Word refers to this as being: "transformed by the renewing of your mind." "Therefore, I urge you, brothers, in view of God's mercy, to offer your bodies as living sacrifices, holy and pleasing to God—this is your spiritual act of worship. Do not conform to the pattern of this world, but be transformed by the renewing of your mind. Then you will be able to test and approve what God's will is—his good, pleasing and perfect will" Romans 12:1-2.

God has the power to change you and your entire attitude and outlook. It would be nice if you could pray a simple prayer and ask God to change you and ZAP, it's done, you are changed. You are now the new you. For some this is probably possible; the people who don't have the 60 pound pack on their backs. They don't have a lot of emotional baggage to lug around. They had a wonderful family experience from birth forward. Their career has been stellar. They have made their share of mistakes but they were equipped to handle them in a mature Christian way. However, that experience would be the exception rather than the rule. Most of us will have to struggle a bit more with our changes than that. Hey, that's OK. Don't disparage those people. Many others are a testament to what God can do and what he continues to do in enabling them to work through their past experiences. God can take you right where you are today and with Jesus' help can give you a totally new life.

8. EXERCISE YOUR RIGHT OF REFUSAL

Go ahead, push yourself. It's time to quit having pity parties and the poor me attitudes. Get up and get moving toward the rest of your life. You may be down but you are not out. Don't quit. Keep going. You reply: "But you just don't know my circumstances and how hard I've had it." You are absolutely right. I don't. But God does and he specializes in doing the impossible. Keep going and keep growing. With God's help you can and will succeed. With his help you can show your money who's boss and get your financial life in order. With his help you can get every aspect of your entire life in order. God wants you to have a lot of success in your life. In order to succeed you may first have to refuse some things.

You have the right of refusal. You have the right to refuse to wallow in self-pity. You have the right to refuse to blame everyone else besides yourself for your problems. You have the right to refuse to blame God for your problems. You have the right to refuse to get depressed and down on yourself. You have the right to rise above your circumstances. You have the right to lay a solid foundation for yourself, your family, and your future. We could all tell our sob stories, but you don't really want that. Get up, take personal responsibility and get with the program of the rest of your life. Pray a prayer right now and ask God to give you the desire to allow him to begin to transform your attitude and outlook on life.

9. LIVE IN THE PRESENT

Learn to live in the present while pressing toward the future. No matter what your situation is today, it can get better. You get to choose which things you will allow to influence your life. You can learn to live in the present with an eye toward the future blessings God is going to give you. This is a huge step forward toward transformation. Paul had learned the successful principle of living in the present with an eye out for the future and the glorious blessings that it offered. God has many blessings in store for you. Begin to pray and ask God to bless you. Ask for present and future blessings.

In James 4:2, God tells us that we don't have certain blessings because we didn't ask for them: "…You do not have, because you do not ask God." Ask God to bless you spiritually, relationally, materially, and financially. Pray and ask for any blessing you need. Redirect your energies and efforts toward having a better present and future.

10. Learn to Make Better Decisions

Everyone makes hundreds of decisions daily. Some are small decisions with little consequence. Others can be huge and can impact a lot of people. The key is that you can learn to make good decisions. Look back on some of your past decisions and try to determine what factors made them turn out to be good or bad decisions.

You will find that most of your good decisions were made after you did the following:
- You sought after the Lord's leadership and followed it
- You researched your options or the situation before deciding
- You talked to wise people about it before deciding
- You did the right thing
- You made an informed decision and didn't look back

Most poor or really bad decisions we make usually do not include those steps. In fact, most poor decisions are made when people act on impulse and don't think things through.

You Can Make Better Decisions

Good decision makers have learned to make a list of all the pros and cons of the decision they are considering. The next time you have a decision to make use the decision making sheet that follows. Prayerfully make a list of the pros and cons of your decision on a piece of paper. Be honest and write down **ALL** the reasons you should and all the reason you should not make that decision. As you go through this process, ask the Lord to guide you. Listen for his promptings. Be still and know that he is God. As you work through this process, it usually becomes pretty obvious what is the right thing for you to do.

Decision Making Sheet

Decision to Consider: *I want to buy a new car.*

Reasons why I SHOULD do this:
I need a new car
I would look good driving it
All my friends have new cars
It would make me more popular
It would be more dependable
I wouldn't be ashamed to drive it
I will get better gas mileage
_____
_____
_____

Reasons why I SHOULD NOT do this:
I can't afford any more payments
There are other things I need worse
I am trying to stop using credit
_____
_____
_____

My Decision:
In light of the things I have considered I have decided to do the following:
_____
_____

In your opinion, what Decision should this Person make?

It is obvious that the person making this decision doesn't need to buy a new car. Why? Look at the reasons they gave for buying a car. For the most part, all the reasons they listed are wrong reasons to buy a new car. Their list also says that they can't afford the payments. It's a no brainer…they need to say no to the new car at this time.

EXTRAORDINARY TIMES CALLS FOR EXTRAORDINARY RESPONSES
Learn to respond to people, events, situations, and things in your life in ways to honor God and in ways that will benefit you and your family the most. Learn to live your own extraordinary life. Celebrate God's love and his many blessings.

We began this chapter reflecting on American heroes Aron Ralston and Captain Chesley B. "Sulley" Sullenberger who made some of the toughest decisions any person could ever be forced to make. Are you willing to make the tough decisions you have needed to make? You know the very decisions I am referring to, for you have been thinking about one or more of them for months, or even years. The reason you haven't made them is fear. Specifically, fear of failure, or fear of their consequences. Deep down you know that your life will not be what you want it to be until you make the tough choices you have been struggling with. Do you have the guts to make them today?

Part 3
Turbo Charge your Money

Chapter 15
God's Promises and Answered Prayers

GOD'S PROMISES

Picture yourself walking along the white sands of Waikiki beach soaking in the warm sunshine as the clear blue water laps at your feet. Think of yourself standing on top of Mt. LeConte gazing across an endless sea of billions of blazing red, yellow, and orange leaves as the cool fall breezes of the Smokey Mountains skim across your face. Envision yourself standing beside the rim of the Grand Canyon watching the hues of the canyon as they are illuminated by the most vibrant sunset you have ever seen.

Because of God's love, every living person on earth has received some of these blessings that God bestows upon all mankind. In addition to being able to enjoy the awesome beauty of God's wonderful creation, God's blessings include such things as our lives themselves, our ability to have relationships and friendships with other people, sunshine, rain, and a myriad of other things as well. The scriptures even say that God's promises are there for everyone to enjoy: "...for he causes his sun to rise on the evil and the good, and sends rain on the righteous and on the unrighteous" Matthew 5:45. God's blessings are available for mankind to enjoy.

God loves us so much that he has reached out to us through his son, Jesus Christ as the greatest blessing of all. He reached out to us as people whom he LOVES and as people with whom he wishes to have an intimate personal relationship. The Bible is filled with promises that God has made directly to his children. Some think that God is motivated to make promises to his children because he feels obligated to bless and take care of them. However, his real motivation for blessing us and for caring for us is his awesome LOVE.

God's promises are like fields full of glistening diamonds waiting for Christians to come and pick them up. The Lord offers his promises to us through his Word, the Bible. His promises offer us hope, inspire confidence in him, motivate us, inspire us to know him more intimately, and give us reasons to live. His promises bless us, infuse us with a sense of well being, lead us to experience God's love, and show us that he genuinely cares for us. Finally, the Lord's promises prepare us for our future in Heaven, and warn us of the realities of Hell and separation from God. If you are a Christian you owe it to yourself to study God's Word and discover the countless promises that are awaiting you.

Within his sovereign power, our all-knowing God sometimes grants his promises and answered prayers to unbelievers. He does this because he loves all people everywhere. He knows in advance that the person receiving his promises or answered prayers will benefit from those blessings. He also knows whether they will one day come to know him as Savior, or will glorify God within their life in some way, either in an obvious or even a not so obvious way.

The greatest promise of all is one that he will keep for anyone at any time if they sincerely ask him and are willing to commit themselves to him. That promise is his promise to accept you into his family and make you a Christian. It is a free gift from God. You can claim this gift for yourself by accepting Jesus as your Savior and Lord.

Answered Prayers

A few years ago a popular song suggested that God sometimes blesses people with gifts of unanswered prayers. Unless God chooses to ignore a Christian's prayer deliberately, he answers every prayer a Christian ever prays. We just may not be getting the answers we are expecting. First, we all tend to think that answered prayers always have to have the answer of: "Yes." Did it ever occur to you that sometimes God answers prayers in other ways? Sometimes he says: "No." At other times he says: "Maybe" or "Later" or "Someday," or he may even give an answer like: "Let me see just how serious you really are about this before I answer your prayer."

How does one go about getting their prayers answered? Again, all prayers are answered, you just may not be receiving the answer you are looking for. Can you imagine what would happen to your child if your only answer was "yes," to every request he or she ever made? "Mommy, may I have a candy bar for breakfast?" "Why, yes sweetheart, go ahead and eat one, you will enjoy it." At the end of the day they ask: "Daddy, may I eat a bowl of ice cream for supper?" "Sure dear, whatever you want." Later, as a teen they say: "Hey dad, I'm going to the mall to shop with my friends, how about giving me $2,000?"

Ridiculous isn't it? The word "NO" has to be in our vocabularies when it comes to rearing a child whom we wish to grow up to become a responsible adult. Guess what. God has the word "NO" in his vocabulary as well. He will not give you every single thing you ask for. He loves you too much.

All this raises another very important question. "Are there things I can do that will encourage God to answer my prayers with more 'YES' answers?" Sure there are, want to know what they are? Following are four principles that apply to God's answering of our prayers.

1. God Answers the Prayers of His Children

First, be a believer, a true born-again Christian. As a child of God, your Heavenly Father wants to hear from you on a daily basis. He also wants to answer your prayers. The following story may help us better understand this principle.

Joe and Kathy are Christians, have been happily married for 20 years, and have two teen-aged kids. Their son Kyle is 17 and their daughter Courtney is 15. Kyle comes in one day and asks to borrow the family car to take his girlfriend to his high school's afternoon football game. Joe talks with Kyle about his date, reviews the ground rules, gives him some money, and hands him the keys to the car while giving him a hug and sending him on his way. Thirty minutes later Courtney comes in and asks her dad for $50. to take with her as she and her mom go to the mall to buy shoes for her school's choir concert. He hands her $60, wishes her well on her shopping trip, gives her a hug, and tells her to treat mom to a latte at the mall.

Feeling rather fulfilled as a father with two great kids, Joe goes outside to work in the back yard for a couple of hours. While he is busy raking leaves his neighbor's son Billy comes over and asks if he can borrow Joe's car to go hang out with his friends on the other side of town. Joe promptly tells him no and explains that he will have to borrow his own father's car.

No sooner than he gets the words out of his mouth another neighbor, Adrian, 13, calls out from across the fence on the other side of the yard and asks Joe to give her $20.00 so she can buy her brother a birthday present. Joe commends her thoughtfulness but refers her to her own parents and tells her no.

What is the difference between these four requests? Relationship. God loves to provide and care for his own children. Why, because they are members of his family, he is their father, he loves them, they love him, and he has a vested interest in them, their well being, and their futures. However, he does not have to answer the prayers of a non-Christian. The key words are: "have to." God doesn't "have to" answer any prayers of someone who is not a believer. However, he can and does choose to answer some of their prayers. He does so out of love and to bless them. It is just that God is under no obligation to "have to" do so.

Neither is he under any obligation to answer prayers you never pray. In the story above, Kyle wouldn't have been able to borrow his dad's car had he not asked to borrow it. His dad knew he needed it but was waiting for him to ask. In fact, the Lord once said: "You want something but don't get it…you do not have, because you do not ask God" James 4:2. Yet God can and does make exceptions and can answer anyone's prayer he chooses in any way he wishes to answer. That is totally up to him and is done according to his will and for his own good reasons.

2. BE IN FELLOWSHIP WITH GOD

This is also simple to illustrate. Ten years have passed and Joe and his wife Kathy still live in the same house and are doing fine in their marriage, their church, their Christian walk, and their careers. They made their share of mistakes, but they generally feel that they have been successful as parents. One major problem bothers them immensely. They have tried and tried but have been unable to resolve it. Kyle, their 27-year-old son, left home soon after he graduated college at age 21 and has chosen to drop completely out of Joe's and Kathy's lives since that time. He never calls, refuses to see his parents, and has basically chosen to remove himself from their lives. Joe and Kathy have tried repeatedly to contact Kyle and express to him their love, but he will have nothing to do with them. Occasionally he contacts his sister Courtney who is now 25 and living on campus while finishing graduate school. Courtney is just the opposite of Kyle. She talks to her parents several times a week, comes over to their house to visit on weekends, and generally showers them with love and honor.

The difference between these two young adults' involvement in their parents lives is: relationship. Courtney is in fellowship with her parents and Kyle is not. Joe and Kathy love both their kids with the same genuine unconditional love. But the relationship with their kids is different. They have a warm and intimate relationship with Courtney, but a cold, aloof relationship with Kyle. Why? Because Courtney has chosen to be close to her parents and Kyle has chosen to distance himself from them.

This story shows the relationship many Christians have with the Lord. Many have a warm and growing relationship with him and he is able to love them back in tangible and practical ways. Other Christians have become enamored with worldly things and have let their relationship slide to the point of being cold and aloof with their Heavenly Father. He still loves them unconditionally and wants to have an intimate relationship with them but they simply do not respond to his expressions of love for them.

How can you have more of your prayers answered? Be in fellowship with God.

3. Learn to Pray within God's Will

Why do we want more "Yes" answers when we pray? Because we want things to work out the way we think they should. After all, we think we know what is best for us, don't we? Most Christians agree that God is sovereign and that he knows the future. A great step toward Christian maturity is taken when a person learns to trust God's answers in prayer. Some think that God will answer any and every prayer with a "YES," so long as it is prayed within his will. That is not always true, for some of God's greatest answers are "No" answers. For instance Ed, a 16-year-old guy prays for a new Corvette for his birthday. God could give him the car. Giving the gift would be no problem. However, God knows everything about 16-year-old guys and fast cars. Because of his great love for the young man, God answers: "No."

Madison, a 22-year-old girl falls in love with someone who is handsome and appears to be such a nice young man. She prays that God will allow them to get married some day. It never happens. Again, God knows the future and answers her prayer with: "No." Again, it is not the answer she was looking for, but God answers: "No," because he wants to spare her from a lifetime of heartache and relational pains.

God always has our best interests at heart as he answers our prayers. Unfortunately, many people think prayer is an exercise of talking God into something. You and I can't talk God into anything. God is God. He is not some bearded cosmic Santa Claus who lets us sit on his knee to try and talk him into giving us something we want for Christmas. We have all seen a child sitting in his mother's shopping cart having a tantrum over a toy or a bag of candy. I have shocking news for some of you. You are that kid who has grown up and is now an adult. Down deep within the recesses of your mind you still think you can talk someone into something and get your way. In fact, it sometimes works. You get mad, have a tantrum, shed some tears, and get what you want.

That ploy does not work with God. He knows ALL the angles and has seen them all a million times. When we pray he gives us what is best for us, not what we think we can talk him into giving us. I for one am glad that God can't be manipulated. You and I can't talk God into anything. Prayer is not designed to convince God to do things for us. Prayer is a God-given gift that God gives to Christians by which we can synchronize our hearts and lives with God's will for our lives. God is going to give you what is best for you. Your most important job in prayer is to get your heart and attitude right with God so that they both line up with his will. When you pray within his will, your prayers will always be answered. "Delight yourself in the Lord and he will give you the desires of your heart" Psalm 37:4.

Some prayers are answered more quickly than others. This calls for another step in Christian maturity. We can be assured that God has never been and will never be late. He always answers prayer at exactly the precise moment it should be answered. He will never answer it before or after that exact time.

4. No Cheating in Prayer

Cheating in prayer is when people pray in order to salve their guilty consciences. They pray just enough to get to feeling a little better. They project upon God exactly what they want to hear him say. They don't really get an answer from God but they go ahead and do exactly what they were asking God to do for them or to grant them. They are basically self-answering their own prayers. They then tell themselves and others that God answered their prayers when he didn't answer them at all. They answered them all by themselves. That exercise is not prayer. It is a game which when played, is played by oneself. God never has, and never would be involved with this kind of sham.

When Jesus prayed in Matthew 26:42 he included the words: "may your will be done." When we pray within God's will we pray for the things we know that God wants us to have. When you pray and honestly want his will to be done he always answers with the answer that is best for you. He loves you that much.

The greatest and most wonderful prayer that one can pray to begin their relationship with God is one that he will answer for anyone at any time if they sincerely ask him and are willing to commit themselves to him. That prayer is his promise to accept you into his family and make you a Christian. It is a free gift from God. You can claim this gift for yourself by asking Jesus to be your savior.

The 4 Spiritual Laws

Dr. Bill Bright, founder of Campus Crusade for Christ, authored a pamphlet about God's wonderful plan for your life. He identified four principles that can lead you to a personal relationship with God. You can read and study these principles for yourself:

Would you like to Know God Personally?

The following message is a message of love and hope. An exciting adventure awaits those who discover these life-changing truths.

The following four principles will help you discover how to know God personally and experience the abundant life He promised.

God's Perspective

God loves you and created you to know Him personally. He has a wonderful plan for your life.

God's Love

"God so loved the world, that He gave His only begotten Son, that whoever believes in Him should not perish, but have eternal life" (John 3:16).

God's Plan

"Now this is eternal life: that they may know you, the only true God, and Jesus Christ, whom you have sent" (John 17:3).

What prevents us from knowing God personally?

Our Condition

People are sinful and separated from God, so we cannot know Him personally or experience His love and plan.

Man is Sinful

"All have sinned and fall short of the glory of God" (Romans 3:23).

People were created to have fellowship with God; but, because of our own stubborn self-will, we chose to go our own independent way and fellowship with God was broken. This self-will, characterized by an attitude of active rebellion or passive indifference, is an evidence of what the Bible calls sin.

People are Separated

"The wages of sin is death" [spiritual separation from God] (Romans 6:23).

This diagram illustrates that God is holy and people are sinful. A great gulf separates the two. The arrows illustrate that people are continually trying to reach God and establish the personal relationship with Him through our own efforts, such as a good life, philosophy, or religion – but we inevitably fail.

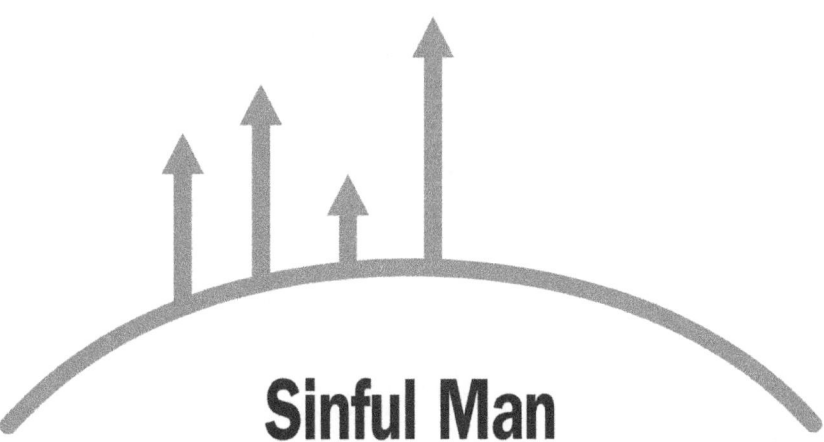

The third principle explains the only way to bridge this gulf...
God's Response

Jesus Christ is God's only provision for our sin. Through Him alone we can know God personally and experience God's love and plan.

He Died in Our Place

"God demonstrates His own love toward us, in that while we were yet sinners, Christ died for us" (Romans 5:8).

He Rose From the Dead

"Christ died for our sins…He was buried…He was raised on the third day according to the Scriptures…He appeared to Peter, then to the twelve. After that He appeared to more than five hundred…" (1 Corinthians 15:3-6).

He is the Only Way to God

"Jesus said to him, 'I am the way, and the truth, and the life; no one comes to the Father, but through Me'" (John 14:6).

This diagram illustrates that God has bridged the gulf that separates us from Him by sending His Son, Jesus Christ, to die on the cross in our place to pay the penalty for our sins.

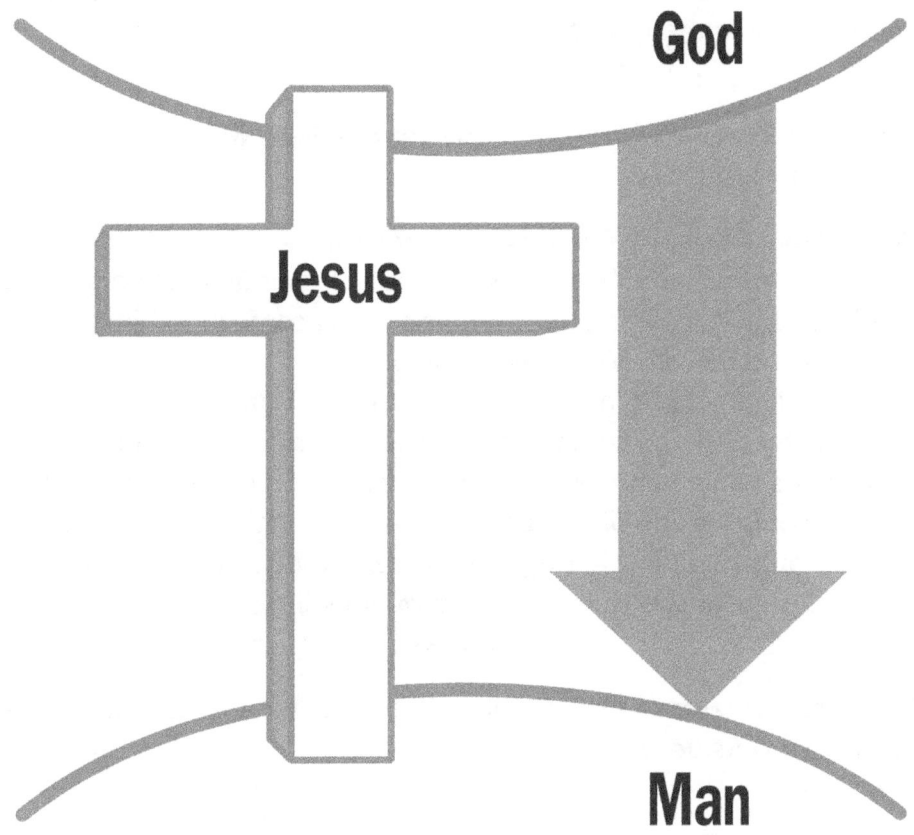

It is not enough just to know these truths...
Our Response

We must individually receive Jesus Christ as Savior and Lord; then we can know God personally and experience His love.

We Must Receive Christ

"As many as received Him, to them He gave the right to become children of God, even to those who believe in His name" (John 1:12).

We Receive Christ Through Faith

"By grace you have been saved through faith; and that not of yourselves, it is the gift of God; not as a result of works that no one should boast" (Ephesians 2:8, 9).

When We Receive Christ, We Experience a New Birth
(Read John 3:1-8).

We Receive Christ by Personal Invitation

[Christ speaking] "Here I am! I stand at the door and knock. If any one hears My voice and opens the door, I will come in to him and eat with him and he with Me." (Revelation 3:20).

Receiving Christ involves turning to God from self (repentance) and trusting Christ to come into our lives to forgive us of our sins and to make us what He wants us to be. Just to agree intellectually that Jesus Christ is the Son of God and that He died on the cross for our sins is not enough. Nor is it enough to have an emotional experience. We receive Jesus Christ by faith, as an act of our will.

These two circles represent two kinds of lives.

A life without Jesus Christ. Self is in the center and on the throne; Christ (†) is outside.

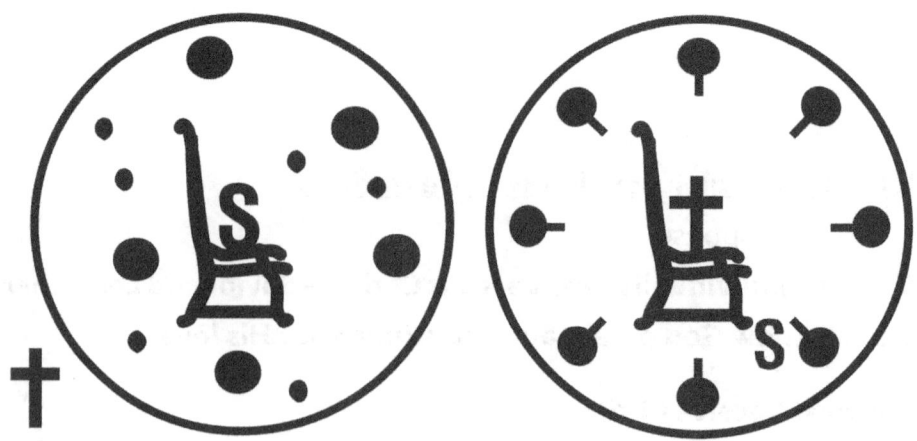

A life entrusted to Christ. Christ is in the center and on the throne, and self yields to Christ.

Which circle best describes your life?
Which circle would you like to have represent your life?

The following explains how you can receive Christ
You Can Receive Christ Right Now by Faith Through Prayer
(Prayer is talking with God)
God knows your heart and is not so concerned with your words as He is with the attitude of your heart. The following is a suggested prayer:

"Lord Jesus, I want to know You personally. Thank You for dying on the cross for my sins. I open the door of my life and receive You as my Savior and Lord. Thank You for forgiving me of my sins and giving me eternal life. Take control of the throne of my life. Make me the kind of person You want me to be."

Does this prayer express the desire of your heart?
If it does, pray this prayer right now, and Christ will come into your life, as He promised.
How to Know That Christ is in Your Life

Did you receive Christ into your life?
According to His promise in Revelation 3:20, where is Christ right now in relation to you? Christ said that He would come into your life and be your friend so you can know Him personally. Would He mislead you? On what authority do you know that God has answered your prayer? (The trustworthiness of God Himself and His Word).

The Bible Promises Eternal Life to All Who Receive Christ
"The witness is this, that God has given us eternal life, and this life is in His Son. He who has the Son has the life; he who does not have the Son of God does not have the life. These things I have written to you who believe in the name of the Son of God, in order that you may know that you have eternal life" (1 John 5:11-13).

Thank God often that Christ is in your life and that He will never leave you (Hebrews 13:5). You can know on the basis of His promise that Christ lives in you and that you have eternal life from the very moment you invite Him in. He will not deceive you.
Do Not Depend on Feelings

The promise of God's Word, the Bible—not our feelings—is our authority. The Christian lives by faith (trust) in the trustworthiness of God Himself and His Word.

Flying a jet can illustrate the relationship among fact (God and His Word), faith (our trust in God and His Word), and feeling (The result of our faith and obedience) (John 14:21).

To be transported by a jet, we must place our faith in the trustworthiness of the aircraft and the pilot who flies it. Our feelings of confidence or fear do not affect the ability of the jet to transport us, they do affect how much we enjoy the trip. In the same way, we as Christians do not depend on feelings or emotions, but we place our faith (trust) in the trustworthiness of God and the promises of His Word.

Now That You Have Received Christ

The moment that you received Christ by faith, as an act of the will, many things happened, including the following:

- Christ came into your life (Revelation 3:20; Colossians 1:27).
- Your sins were forgiven (Colossians 1:14).
- You became a child of God (John 1:12).
- You received eternal life (John 5:24).
- You began the great adventure for which God created you (John 10:10; 2 Corinthians 5:17; 1 Thessalonians 5:18).

Can you think of anything more wonderful that could happen to you than receiving Christ? Would you like to thank God in prayer right now for what He has done for you? By thanking God, you demonstrate your faith.

To enjoy your new life to the fullest...
Suggestions for Christian Growth

Spiritual growth results from trusting Jesus Christ. "The righteous man shall live by faith" (Galatians 3:11). A life of faith will enable you to trust God increasingly with every detail of your life, and to practice the following:

- G   Go to God in prayer daily (John 15:7).
- R   Read God's Word daily (Acts 17:11); begin with the Gospel of John.
- O   Obey God moment by moment (John 14:21).
- W   Witness for Christ by your life and words (Matthew 4:19; John 15:8).
- T   Trust God for every detail of your life (1 Peter 5:7).
- H   Holy Spirit—allow Him to control and empower your daily life and witness (Galatians 5:16, 17; Acts 1:8).

Remember

Your walk with Christ depends on what you allow Him to do in and through you empowered by the Holy Spirit, not what you do for Him through self effort.

Fellowship in a Good Church

God's Word instructs us not to forsake "the assembling of ourselves together" (Hebrews 10:25). Several logs burn brightly together; but put one aside on the cold hearth and the fire goes out. So it is with your relationship with other Christians.

If you do not belong to a church, do not wait to be invited. Take the initiative; call the pastor of a nearby church where Christ is honored and His Word is preached. Start this week, and make plans to attend regularly.

Find a church in your area where God's Word is taught and obeyed

Find out how to enjoy the friendship and encouragement of other Christians on your campus (Contact CCFI at www.campuscrusadeforchrist.com.)

Have You Heard of the Four Spiritual Laws? written by Bill Bright C 1965-2009. Campus Crusade for Christ Intl (CCCI) and Bright Media Foundation (BMF). All rights reserved. Used by permission. No part of this work may be changed in any way or reproduced without written permission from CCCI and BMF.

CLAIM GOD'S PROMISES FOR YOURSELF

Now that you have read the details about God's wonderful plan for your life, I encourage you to allow Jesus to come into your life and become your Savior and Lord. Find a good church and begin fellowshipping with other Christians in your area. Claim the awesome promises of God for your very own. Begin reading about his promises in the New Testament book of John's Gospel. Read and meditate upon one of its 21 chapters each day. Spend some quiet moments alone with the Lord in prayer each day. Ask him to lead you and to bless you and your family.

How does this relate to showing your money who's boss? When you allow Jesus to be the Lord of your life, EVERY single aspect of your life will come into order…including your money and finances.

Chapter 16
Show Your Money Who's Boss

Virtually everyone has seen a two-year-old child in the grocery store having a tantrum and gaining control over his mom or dad. The parent usually gives in and buys the toy, the box of cereal, or the candy they are screaming about. The child knows that he is in control and he takes advantage of his power over his parents for all he can get out of them. It may be cute when the child is two years old, but what happens when the child turns 15? It is spelled…disaster. If you don't have control when the child is two, what will you do when he turns 15? You need to get a plan together fast. To sharpen your child rearing skills, check out James Dobson's: **The New Strong-Willed Child**.

Who hasn't seen a large dog "walking" its owner? You can see this scene unfold in almost any city park or walking trail. A huge 100 pound dog strains with all its might. He is straining against all the force his owner can muster while being tethered to the end of a leash. Bruno pulls his owner all over the park. Major frustration shows his master's face. Bruno is the pack leader, and he knows it. He proudly drags his owner along asserting his dominance, and proudly showing off his owner to all the other dogs in the park. One look at the poor sap, and you laughingly remark to your spouse: "Looks like he is in serious need of a visit from the Dog Whisperer." The truth is that you are right. He is in need of all the help he can get. The sad reality is that he probably will continue to allow Bruno to drag him all over the park for the next 10 years or so. He sentences himself to 10 years of total frustration with his dog.

That is how many allow their money to function in their lives. Their money controls them and drags them around to all the places it chooses to go. The owner simply holds onto the leash. In a perfect world you would always be in total control of your money. You would make perfect decisions every time you made a financial decision or spend some of your hard-earned cash. Being perfect is not realistic for anyone, but you can avoid the traps many people have fallen into. While you won't reach perfection on earth, there is one major goal you can realistically expect to reach. You can learn to control your money instead of allowing your money to control you. Too many people have lost any semblance of control over their money. Their money is controlling them.

For some people, money management skills are similar to the-two-year old kid who is having a tantrum. Your money demanded control and you gave in. Others feel as though they are like an out-of-control dog-owner who is being pulled around the park. Your money screams for you to buy something…anything, just spend. Much of the time you give in. Someone will win this conflict. It will either be you or your money and your spending habits. Only you can decide who is in control.

Are you spending more and enjoying it less? Do you have this gut-feeling that you are not in control of your finances, your finances are controlling you? Are you sick and tired of always being broke? Do you constantly wonder where your money went? Do you feel that your finances are totally out of control? If you answered yes to any of these questions THERE IS HOPE FOR YOU!

You Can Show your Money who's BOSS

When I refer to your money being in control I am referring to your money management practices and your spending habits. If you allow your spending habits to win, you will continue doing what you have always done. Nothing will change. If you decide to take charge of your money management skills, you will need to reorient your spending habits. You will need to move from an impulsive spending approach toward a disciplined and goal-oriented approach to spending. If you do this you will soon begin to see that you are getting more bangs for your bucks, and you will end up having a lot more bucks for the things you really need.

Poor spending habits are not a function of being poor or rich. Many poor people have great spending habits, they just happen to be poor. Many rich people have poor spending habits; their poor spending is usually masked by the fact that they have a lot more money than the average person.

Consider the number of highly paid professional athletes who receive multi-million dollar salaries and bonuses while playing sports. Many of them end up in retirement with little or nothing because of their poor spending practices. They had it, they spent it, they enjoyed it, and now they regret it. For a guy to have earned in excess of $100 million and retire with nothing says that he had some lousy spending and money management practices.

Money Can Be Like a Drug Addiction

One of the saddest things you can see is a person whose life is controlled by drugs. Whether one's drug of choice is alcohol, marijuana, crack cocaine, or methamphetamine, drugs can rob a person of the essence of life. An addict lives to get high. Every waking moment is spent thinking about how and when they are going to get their next fix. It may be a few drinks in a bar or it may be smoking a joint in the car after work. It could be a crack pipe or a hit of speed. They live for the next high. Little else matters, for their life revolves around drugs.

Money and the temporary happiness, thrills, and excitement it can provide are like a drug addiction for some people. Money addiction manifests itself in many ways. For some, the thrill is in earning money. Accumulating money in a money-market fund or IRA is the appeal for others. For many, their thrill is found in spending money and relishing in the powerful high that spending provides. A lavish lifestyle is the high that many others strive to attain. Money can rob a person of the essence of life. Some people's entire lives revolve around money. They spend every waking moment thinking of new ways to earn, accumulate, hoard, spend, or enjoy their money. The problem is this: they are wasting much of their valuable time and energy chasing the illusive pot-of-gold at the end of the rainbow. For, once they find it, they realize that what they have found is really nothing but a hollow chocolate Easter bunny full of nothing more than emptiness.

When it comes to gaining control over your money one of the most important things you can do is regain control over your spending. That is one of the major steps in showing your money who's boss.

Developing Good Spending Habits

Most people who have achieved success in managing their finances have been able to do so because they have developed a clear understanding of how and when to spend money. Like a tightrope walker, they have achieved a great sense of balance when it comes to spending money. They have learned: How to spend. When to spend. Why to spend. And, What to spend their money on. They have also learned: How not to spend. When not to spend. Why not to spend. And, What not to spend their money on.

People with this great sense of balanced spending were born that way weren't they? It may surprise you, but NO, they were not born with their excellent sense of balanced spending. They had to learn that behavior or skill. They may have started learning balanced spending as a two year old kid who learned that pitching a tantrum in the grocery store will NOT earn him his toy, or cereal, or candy. His parents didn't give in to his every whim or whimper.

Those parents taught their children the value of money and let them learn the value of money by making some mistakes along the way. Great spenders learned how to spend money. They may have been exactly where you were when they started on their journey of learning how to manage their spending. Great spenders have learned the secrets of controlling their money and their emotions instead of allowing their money to control them.

Where are you in the spending equation? You may have it all figured out and may be having such success that you could teach others how to control their spending. Or, you may be searching for answers and need help gaining control over your spending. Some will want to learn how to spend less, while a few others will want to learn how to spend more. No, that was not a misprint…some people actually do need to learn how to spend more money. "I sure wish I had that problem," you say. "OK, I don't have that problem. I need to learn how to spend LESS money," you say. There are definite steps you and your family can take to begin spending less money.

When Your Money Runs Low or Runs out You Have Options

You can either: 1. Live on what you earn. 2. Spend less. 3. Earn more money. 4. Spend money you do not have and hope that you can pay it back later...credit card debt. That is so simple that a Harvard MBA can figure that out. Spending is out of control for many people. Since you are unable to print more money or strike oil in your back yard, you may wish to consider these options.

1. Live on what You Earn

What a novel concept. Who ever heard of that? Living on what you earn is the best option. It is not necessarily where we would like to be. Everyone would like to earn more money than it takes to pay all of their living expenses. Everyone would like to have money left over at the end of every pay period. The harsh reality is this...most people don't live there. Too many live beyond what they earn. They buy things that they couldn't otherwise afford by charging them to their credit cards. Most people either live up to or down to their income level. With a measure of self-control you can retrain yourself to live on your present income by spending less than you make.

2. Spend Less

Almost everyone could learn to get by on less than they earn. Consider this hypothetical situation. A friend you work with has an accident and becomes totally disabled. Since his accident happened while he was working, he now draws a disability check that totals 50% of what he was earning a few months ago. He is forced to spend less money because he has less money. He finds ways to cut back that he had never even thought about. Your friend from work learned to cut back on spending because he was forced to do so by a horrible accident. If we are forced to live on less, we can do it. It's just that we don't want to live on less. You can make the decision to cut back and spend less because you choose to do so.

3. Earn More Money

Earning more money is easy IF you can get a higher paying job, get a raise, take a second or third job, or your spouse goes back to work. Answer this question: "Why do I need more money?" Having more money so that I can buy more stuff is not the best answer. Having extra time for yourself and time with your family is of far more value than just having more stuff. If you need more money for the basic necessities of life or to pay off your debts, that is a better reason than just wanting more stuff. If you need more money you do have options. They include a higher paying job, taking a second part-time job, your spouse going to work, or your working-aged kids helping defray household expenses. More money can be a good thing so long as your priorities are in line with what you are trying to accomplish.

4. SPEND NOW AND PAY LATER

You see something you want and you have to have it. You whip out the plastic and give it a swipe. You feel great. You deserved it. Three weeks later the bill comes and you don't have the money to pay for it so you make the minimum payment and let the balance slide until later. That is precisely how millions of Americans build huge outstanding balances on credit cards. They build a $10,000 balance one purchase at a time. Spending money you do not have and hoping to pay it back later is a dead end street. Too many people are living there today. There is help for you if this describes your situation.

Can you believe how much less your parents or grandparents earned than what you earn? Sure, the dollar was worth more back then, and things did cost less than they do today. But their standard of living was better than that of today. In addition to the Harvard MBA, the average Joe on the street has figured this out.

THINGS YOUR GREAT GRANDPARENTS NEVER HAD

Consider four things you have that none of your great grandparents and many of your grandparents never had. 1. A home equity line of Credit. 2. A 401k. 3. A collection of credit cards. 4. A huge amount of debt. How did your grandparents get by without these things and how did their type of economy function? Actually they were usually better off than the average American today. There are several reasons why. People lived on what they earned. They paid for things when they bought them. They were more sensible when it came to borrowing. They practiced deferred gratification or impulse control. Those are fancy terms that mean they didn't rush out and charge their version of the Xbox to their credit card when it first hit the market. They saved up for it and bought it when they had the money. What a boring life, and yes, what a novel idea. When your grandparents borrowed money, they borrowed only what they could pay back. They borrowed money for things like a house, a car, or to start a business. They didn't run down to the local shopping center and charge everything they wanted without any concern for when they would pay it back.

Where it All Started

Where did we go wrong and get up to our eyeballs in debt? When did things change? Things began changing when banks saw the potential for billions in profits and put gazillions of credit cards into the hands of American consumers. Things began changing when the folks on Madison Avenue realized that they could make billions by creating advertisements that tempted people to begin spending money that they didn't have. Most importantly, things began changing when people stopped living within their means. Living within one's means is simple. It means: Living on what you earn. It does not mean living on what you earn plus what you can borrow or charge on a credit card. This is something that an increasing number of Americans are now practicing with reckless abandon.

That's enough of all that. Let's move on to where many are living today and what you can do to help improve your situation.

Spending Categories

Here are examples of different types of spending:

Mandatory...buying things you must have to live: basic food, clothing, shelter

Discretionary...buying things you want but don't necessarily need: big screen TV, new car, new iphone

Excessive...spending beyond what you can afford: "I know I can't afford it, but I'll come up with some way to pay for it later."

Impulsive...you hadn't planned on buying it but you saw it, you wanted it, you bought it

Deficit...you don't have the money but you spend anyway, you put it on your credit card

Therapeutic...you spend because it makes you feel good, powerful, and in control

Out of control...you can't stop spending, your spending controls you

Compulsive…you want to stop excessive spending but deep inside you have this feeling that you can't do it by yourself

14 Ways to Show Your Money Who's Boss

The doctor told the patient who was sick and needed an injection to get well: "It's going to hurt a little, but here we go." Any time you have to show your money who's boss, it is going to hurt. The hurt comes from having to change your spending habits and disciplining yourself to do without something you once enjoyed but now you have decided that you can't have. There are some definite steps you can take to cut back on your personal or your family's spending. There are FAR MORE THAN FOURTEEN WAYS to show your money who's boss. These fourteen categories are given as mere starting points. Look at your personal spending habits and identify areas where you need to show your money who's boss and tame your personal money monsters. Add as many, or as few of your own as you wish.

Read these, pray about them, think them over, discuss them with your family, and consider applying those that would improve your personal financial situation. As you read and discuss your spending you will discover other ways you can cut back on your spending. If you discover that you are experiencing spending that is out of control, please seek help from a professional financial advisor or counselor.

Housing

If your house is paid for, celebrate and continue living there. If you are in a house you can't afford to keep, sell it and move to a smaller house or to an apartment. If you are in an upside-down mortgage, where you owe more than your house is worth, seek advice from a trained financial counselor. They may advise you to keep your house if it is possible for you to continue making the payments. If you decide that you have to sell it and are fortunate enough to sell it you may take a hit on its value. Depending upon the housing market in your area you might expect to take a big loss. Some people have taken hits of up to 25% and more. Talk with an honest, knowledgeable, and reputable real estate agent before you decide to do anything. Unless you have to take a loss, don't take it. A 25% loss in value translates to a dollar loss of $25,000 on each $100,000 of your house's value. That is real money.

If you can't possibly keep your house you may have to let it go regardless of the loss you incur. A word of CAUTION: should you choose to default on your mortgage, you will take a mega hit on your credit worthiness. Hey, but we are talking financial survival here. Sometimes you have to do what you have to do to keep afloat. Do yourself a giant favor and talk to a reputable real estate agent before you decide to default on your mortgage. They may advise you to let it go back to the mortgage company, but they could offer other suggestions that could allow you to avoid default.

Develop New Spending Habits

Stop all Unnecessary Spending. You will have to define what "unnecessary" means for you. We are talking about the "bare bones" approach here. Don't buy anything you don't have to have. Buy as many bargains as you possibly can. You can save a significant amount of money over the course of a year by shopping consignment and other discount stores, bargain food stores, and others. Don't buy the 52-inch big screen you have been wanting. Use your old computer for another couple of years. Wear your clothes and shoes longer than you normally would. Drive your car another year or two. Find other ways to use what you have and cut out all but essential spending.

Keep Working

Do everything possible to keep your job and the income it provides. Depending on where you live and how the jobs market is in your area this may be the toughest part of all.

Sell One of Your Cars

Again, we are talking about taking drastic measures here. If you own more than one vehicle, sell one and pay off the one remaining. If you have a vehicle that is paid for and you have finished making its payments, keep that vehicle. The least expensive and most economical transportation you will ever own is the reliable car with no payments. A good rule of thumb: "If it's paid for drive it." Have it repaired if you have to, but drive it. Don't get some foolish notion that you need to trade cars to get better gas mileage. How many people have bought a newer car and financed if for tons more money than they can afford in order to get five more miles per gallon. Do you know how long you would have to drive that new car just to break even on what you would have spent on gasoline? Try 100 years or more. Of course I'm exaggerating, but you get the point.

Don't lease a car. Generally, it is a rip-off. Buy a cheaper used car, preferably from an honest individual owner who is selling through the newspaper, or an honest dealer recommended by a trusted friend. Are you already in a lease? In many cases you have options. Check your lease agreement before you do anything. You may be able to break your lease. However, if your contract specifies that you can't break your lease without an exorbitant cash penalty, then your only option is to drive the car until you have paid out the terms of the lease, and then buy a cheaper used car. Save up and pay cash for your next car. Saving up the cash will make you a better buyer because you will really evaluate your decision before you spend your money.

CARPOOL

Carpool to work, school, church, shopping, and on errands. Let your kids carpool to football or cheerleader practice and let them ride the bus to school and back. How much time and gasoline does one spend on driving Michael and Mason to school and then waiting in line while picking them up when school is out?

CLOTHING

Learn to shop for bargains, stop buying clothes at expensive retail establishments. Adopt this silly, but effective motto: "If it's paid for, wear it." Wear what you have. Forget the $500 designer shoes, suits, and purses. Virtually stop all spending on clothes. If you are in a desperate financial situation try trading clothes with family or friends. Do you have growing kids who need clothes and shoes? Consider trading hand-me-down clothes with friends who have children. Shop the thrift shops. Guaranteed: you won't be stylish at all times, but you will be getting out of debt and getting your feet back on solid financial ground.

FOOD

Buy store brands, use coupons, and take advantage of the buy-one-get-one-free and coupon doubling days. Start cooking meals from scratch instead of buying foods that are the "heat and serve" variety.

GET OUT OF DEBT

From time to time you may wish to review the timeless principles of getting out of debt were outlined in Chapter 11.

CUT THE CABLE OR SATELLITE

Have a ceremony and tell it goodbye. You will miss some of your favorite programs but you will be saving money and you will have more time with which to do other things.

CUT THE CELL PLAN

You may be surprised to find out just how much you spend per year on cell phone service. Let's see, $95.00 per month for 12 months equals $1,140. If you cut your plan and your minutes actually used back to $30.00 per month you will save $780.00 per year. "But I can't live without my cell phone and my text messaging." We all have to make difficult choices. The choices you make are up to you.

RENT MOVIES

Now how much did you say it costs your family to go to the movies at your favorite theater? A movie and snacks can easily cost more than $50.00 for a family. You can rent many of the same movies on the Internet for $1.00. This can save your family a lot of money over the span of a year.

CUT BACK ON EATING OUT

Now he has really started meddling. Let's see, $50.00 per week for 52 weeks equals $2,600.00. Reacquaint yourself with that large rectangular box in your kitchen called a stove. "Hello stove, my name is_____, we are going to get to know one another really well over the next few months." Start with the simplest dishes you can think of and work your way up from there. Tell your family that your while your name is not "Julia," you are going to be cooking and saving the family some money. Learn to cook their favorites, and enlist their help with cooking and washing the pots, pans, and dishes. Another plus: the foods you prepare at home are probably a lot healthier for you as well.

Low Budget Vacations or Skip a Vacation

People usually charge their vacations and never really stop to think how much they are spending. Airfare, rental car, hotel, food, attractions, and other entertainment can cost a family of four anywhere from $2,000—$4,000 dollars for a week of fun in the sun. Everyone needs a break from time to time, but consider staying at home and visiting the local sights or going to a relative's house for a few days and save a ton of money.

Reign in Impulsive Spending

Other

These ideas were just starter ideas. You can think of many additional ways to reduce your spending and save money. Talk to your family and get their feedback. Spending less will not be a lot of fun but it can help you get through your personal financial crisis and will help prepare for better times that lie ahead.

A Good Starting Point

The late Larry Burkett was the pioneer in the Christian financial ministry movement. Larry was the first to begin teaching solid financial principles from the Bible, including advocating a cash system for all payments. He taught people to set up an envelope system whereby one would divide his paycheck into the various payments that need to be paid. Larry's system taught people to designate an envelope for each payment such as tithe, house payment, utilities, car, groceries, clothing, entertainment, medical insurance, life insurance, and so forth. His envelope system helped tens of thousands of people begin to budget their monies and live within their means by advocating spending cash for everything and rejecting the use of credit cards. Since a majority of people are using debit cards today, the same system could still be employed by using envelopes that contain spending or balance sheets to record all expenditures. This may require a bit of ingenuity and record keeping, but it will work. Burkett's materials are still available today and you may wish to explore for yourself. Check them out at: www.crown.org.

DECIDING WHO'S BOSS: YOU OR YOUR MONEY

Decide who's boss, you or your money. Until you decide that YOU are the BOSS over your money, your money will control you and your life. Once you decide that you will be the boss over your money you will have to work to keep it under control. If you fail to keep it under control, you will find that things can spin out of control rather quickly, and your money and your finances will be out of control once again.

One of the best way to show your money who's boss is to decide that you are going to manage your money. Managing your money means just that. You are in charge. You are the manager. You decide everything about your money. You decide: 1. How you earn it. 2. What you will buy with it. 3. Where, when, and how you will spend it. 4. To whom you will pay some of it.

Managing your money is like the managing a baseball team. You decide who will play, what position they will play, how many innings they will play, the order they will bat, and when they will have their next practice. You also decide things like who will pitch, and when a runner should attempt to steal a base. A manager manages his team by making decisions about the game. Managing is dynamic in nature. Not every game is managed in exactly the same way. Neither is every game managed before the game begins. The manager makes many decisions before the game begins, but he makes many more decisions as the game progresses. His in-game decisions are based upon what happens during the course of the game. These managerial decisions are merely adjustments that are made as the game is being played. These adjustments are made with one purpose in mind: win the game.

The same is true of managing money. You make many decisions before your paycheck is deposited. These decisions are made in advance as you budget where your money will be spent. You will also have to make many other important decisions as the game progresses…emergency spending decisions, spending adjustments, and unplanned spending decisions.

Before you can reach financial success you will have to get your spending in control. This means that you control your spending habits. You make the decisions about how and where and upon what to spend your money. If you don't step up to the plate and take responsibility to control your money someone else will control it for you. "Who could do that?" you ask." Those who would control your money are your creditors…those to whom you owe money. "The rich rule over the poor, and the borrower is servant to the lender" Proverbs 22:7. Others who would control your money are dear old familiar friends, your old spending habits. Some of those old habits will have to be broken. If they are not dealt with and dealt with decisively, they will keep raising their ugly heads and will cost you dearly.

Controlling your own money and being in charge of your finances requires a lot of maturity, self-discipline, and self-control. You can do it. You may call upon the Lord and his Word to be your primary resources. Couple them with Christian books like this and others and you will be able to equip yourself for whatever lies ahead. Are you ready to begin showing your money who's boss?

The next chapter will challenge some to a depth they have never been before. Warning, it is not for the faint of heart!

Chapter 17
Receiving God's Wildest XTreme Blessings

CROSSING NIAGARA ON A TIGHTROPE

XTreme Sports have swept across modern American culture. However, they have been around longer than many people think. Had you been standing on the banks of the Niagara River in 1859, just downstream from the falls, you could have witnessed one of the most XTreme sporting events in human history. Jean-Francios Gravelet, better known as Charles Blondin, crossed the river by walked across on a tightrope while carrying his manager, Harry Colcord, on his back. Had they fallen into the river it would have meant certain death for both men as they would have fallen 200 feet into swift currents. The Great Blondin crossed tightropes over the Niagara River scores of times over a period of several years. He crossed the rope while blindfolded, in a sack, on stilts, at night, and with a bicycle. On one occasion, he reportedly asked the crowd, that had gathered to watch his crossing, for a volunteer to cross the river with him. The catch was that Blondin would walk the rope while pushing his passenger across the river in a wheelbarrow. He had no takers. During his career he never once fell into the river and performed his tightrope skills all across Europe before dying in England in his 70s.

LIVING ON THE EDGE

XTreme sports like XTreme skiing, motocross, skydiving, snowboarding, kayaking, mountain climbing, skateboarding, and many others test almost every aspect of a person's existence. They push a person to the limits of physical, mental, emotional, and spiritual endurance. They also test a person's wisdom, faith, knowledge, concentration, level of trust, fear, and just about everything else imaginable.

These qualities literally push a person's body, mind, and spirit to the limits. XTreme sports are not for the weak at heart but are reserved for the brave, the strong, the determined, and the dedicated sports enthusiast. People are in love with this thrill seeking phenomenon.

XTREME CHRISTIANITY

God issued a dare. That is almost unheard of in the Bible. His dare was so XTreme that it will push some of you to the very edge of your spiritual lives. It will rock you at the core of your existence because it will demand:
- XTreme Will
- XTreme Faith
- XTreme Obedience
- XTreme Sacrifice
- XTreme Relationship

These five XTremes will be rewarded with: XTreme Blessings.

GOD'S XTREME DARE TO HIS PEOPLE

God's dare to today's Christians is found in the Old Testament book of Malachi 3:10: where God says: "Test me in this, and see if I will not throw open the floodgates of heaven and pour out so much blessing that you will not have room enough for it."

"Now, let me get this straight. First, God is issuing a dare, and second, God is promising the wildest, XTreme blessings to those who accept his dare." Right in both instances; read on. God's dare basically asks Christians to "put their money where their mouth is." It is one thing to talk a good game. It is something entirely different to actually prove it by actions and deeds. Many Christians talk a good game about how much they love the Lord, how much faith they have in him, and how much God blesses them. It is something different to be able to back it up with true, undeniable actions.

HOW MUCH DO YOU TRUST GOD WITH YOUR MONEY?

Possible answers include:
1. "Why, I trust him totally."
2. "I trust him quite a bit."

3. "I honestly didn't know that he wanted me to trust him with my money."

4. "I don't trust him with my money at all."

5. Fill in your own answer.

One way to prove to yourself how much you trust God with your money is to look at your checkbook or bank statement and see how much of your money you have given to the Lord. XTreme Christianity exhibits the following: XTreme Will, XTreme Faith, XTreme Obedience, XTreme Sacrifice, and XTreme Relationship. Your checkbook or bank statement is a good barometer of just how XTreme your Will, Faith, Obedience, Sacrifice, and Relationship are in your Christian walk.

There are at least a gazillion reasons why people don't give their money to God. Many sound reasonable. Most can be justified. All can be rationalized. "I knew that you were going to get around to money somewhere in this book." Yes, you were right. However, there is one difference that separates this book's addressing the subject of money from others. This writer is not asking you to send him a cent of your money. He is asking you to invest your money in God's work through your local church.

How Much does God Want?

You may be surprised to find out that God really doesn't want or need your money. What he really wants is far more valuable than money. He wants you to surrender your will, your faith, your obedience, and your relationship to him. He is asking you to sacrifice. We are talking XTremes here. I guarantee that these will push many of you to your limit. Oh, but they are worth it.

In the verse quoted above, God was daring his people to test him. His dare involved their money…specifically their money which they were NOT giving to him. In fact, they were keeping most of their money for themselves and giving little if any to God. God was so incensed by their lack of faith, obedience, and sacrifice that he referred to them as robbers. They were actually guilty of robbing God of the tithes and offerings they should have been giving him. He asked them to: "Bring the whole tithe into the storehouse."

That is when he issued his dare to them. He challenged them at the very core of their existence. He was saying: (my paraphrase,)

"Hey Christian, test me by giving me the first 10% of your income. Test me by exercising your will, faith, trust, obedience, and sacrifice. Stand back and watch what I will do for you. Watch me; I will blow you away with XTreme blessings. Come on, I dare you!" God is unapologetically asking his people to give him a tithe of their incomes. What is a tithe? A tithe is 10% of a person's total income. So if a tithe is 10%, what is an offering? An offering is any amount given to God above the 10% figure.

By now you may be talking to yourself: "Is God saying that I should give him 10% of my total income," you ask? Then you answer your own question: "No way, that's crazy, that's TOO XTreme." Uh-oh, you just said the "X" word.

Remember: XTreme Will, XTreme Faith, XTreme Obedience, XTreme Sacrifice, and XTreme Relationship equals XTreme blessings. "OK, OK God, you have proven your point and I see what you are saying, and I am beginning to agree that you are right. But how in the world do I start tithing to you? You know that I may lose my job, or my house, plus I already am drowning in credit card debt. Where am I supposed to get the money to give you?"

How Do I Get to That Level?

1. Some can give 10% immediately, no problem. You need to talk this over with God, with your spouse, with your family, and then start giving 10% next Sunday.

2. Others may be in the fight of your financial lives. You are in total financial chaos and are struggling to survive. You can't pay your rent or house payment, can't buy enough food for the kids, and can't pay your monthly bills. Talk this over with God, with your spouse, with your family, and then put your faith in action next Sunday. In the book of Luke, Chapter 15, a poor widow gave her last two coins to God. Though the value of her gift was less than one penny in today's currency, Jesus said that she had given more than all the others combined who had given their offerings on that day. Your best option is to go "cold-turkey," and start giving 10% of what you have to the Lord and test him to the limit.

3. Many are in the middle. You are living comfortably. You are not in danger of losing your job, your house, or your car. You have moder-

ate credit card debt and always pay your bills on time. You need to talk this over with God, with your spouse, with your family, and then start giving 10% next Sunday.

THAT IS JUST TOO RADICAL

"That is just too radical," you say. You are right. It is too radical for many people. But it is what God asks Christians to do. What's more, there are literally millions of Christians worldwide who are giving 10% and more of their incomes from every paycheck to God every single payday. Giving to God is a wonderful investment that offers greater rewards than any stock or mutual fund on earth.

"But 10% is really just too radical." you say. You had better be glad that God is not as radical as the IRS. What if God asked you to give him 15%, 25%, 28%, 33%, or 35% of your total income as required by the IRS tax brackets? Talking about radical? God only asks you for a mere 10%. Wow, that's not much at all is it?

It has been estimated that the average American pays approximately 42% of their total income in Federal, State, Local, FICA, Medicare, Real Estate, Gasoline, sales, and other taxes. That equals $42,000 of every $100,000. Approximately 20% of the prices we pay for consumer goods are hidden taxes. With that figured in it is easy to see where the 42% figure is derived.

TAKE A BREAK

It is Tuesday night, you have had a tough day at work and you really don't want to face the kitchen when you get home. You call your spouse and arrange to pick up the kids and meet at your favorite restaurant for dinner. You order, you relax, you eat a tasty meal, you fill a to-go box, and you pay your $59 check. The last thing you do is leave your waitress a $10 tip as you leave the restaurant and go home to relax and feed the dog and cat. Let's see, you gave her a 16.9% tip. She certainly deserved it because of the excellent food and service, plus she probably has a family at home depending upon her income. You did a good thing.

Why do we complain when God asks us to give him 10% of our incomes? "Well, that's different," you say. How is it different? He is the Sovereign King of Kings and Lord of Lords, Creator of the universe and

Savior. Why is it that we stiff God his 10% and tip the waitress 16.9%? Is it because we were never taught this; or could it be that Satan has blinded us to giving? Is it because we are deliberately disobedient to God, or are we simply that selfish or careless or stubborn?

"But I give to United Way and the Red Cross, does that not count for something?" It sure does count for something…its called charitable giving. Many charities do a lot of good for a lot of people and that is great. However, they are not God and they don't necessarily represent him or his will in all that they do with their monies. When God asks us to give he asks that we give to him, not to a charity. Give to God first and then give to the charity of your choice.

When God asks you to give 10% to him he is talking about investing your 10% in his work through your local church. If you don't have a local church, pray about it and ask God to lead you to a congregation where you can get involved in service to him. Give your money to that congregation once you have found it. If you are a member of a local church and it is not meeting your spiritual needs, check and see whether you are the reason it is not meeting them. If you are not the problem and you are convinced that the church is not what it is supposed to be, then you need to pray and ask God to lead you to a loving church where you can serve him and invest your money in that congregation. Others will say something like: "I just don't agree with what they are doing at my church and I'm not sure I can trust them with my money." When your gift of money leaves your hand it becomes God's responsibility. You no longer are responsible to account for it. I think you can trust God to see that he deals with his money in the proper way.

XTreme Blessings

Just what are the XTreme blessings God is talking about in these following verses? "I will prevent pests from devouring your crops, and the vines in your fields will not cast their fruit, says the Lord Almighty. Then all the nations will call you blessed, for yours will be a delightful land," says the LORD Almighty" Malachi 3:11-12.

These verses were originally written to a people who lived in an agrarian society. Not many of us are farmers, so what are the principles from these verses for us if we are not farmers today?

By extension they would have the following meaning for the 21st century. I will protect you. I will look after your best interest in every aspect of life. I will bless you with countless blessings. I will prosper you and all you do for me. I will bless and prosper your career, your business dealings, and your use of money. I will be there for you when you encounter troubles. I will comfort you when you need comfort. I will see that other people will bless you and recognize your prosperity. There, you have 10 examples of God's blessings. There are many many more.

XTreme blessings mean that God will bless you more and more and more. The more you trust him and rely upon him and obey him and love him and bless him and honor him, the sweeter your relationship with him becomes and the more you will be blessed by him. Someone once stated it so simply and elegantly when they said: "You can't outgive God."

Want more blessings? Then ask God for them. Want to be blessed in XTreme ways? Then do some XTreme giving.

10/90 Principle Revisited

In Chapter 12 we talked about the important principle of paying yourself first. Investing or saving 10% of your income and living on the remaining 90%. Remember? Now we kick it to an XTreme level, which is far more radical than that. This principle is not for the weak or faint of heart. Here it is:

The XTreme Principle 10/10/80

At this point, it probably needs little explanation. Plus, I promise there is not another 10/10 principle coming up in a subsequent chapter. But just in case someone missed it, here is an explanation of this XTreme principle.

XTreme Principle 10/10/80

Give God the first 10%
Pay yourself the second 10%
Live off the remaining 80%

That is the 10/10/80 principle. Admittedly, this is almost over the top for most people. Many of you will say something like: "Hey, I think

I could have handled the 10/90 principle, but this is just too much." Yes, it may be XTreme XTreme. But it is the truth. And, once you get yourself set up to make it happen, you will be blown away with blessings. I know that it works, because my family and I have been following this principle for a number of years. Actually, there are millions of people worldwide who have committed to this principle and are being blessed immensely.

Your 100 Fold Increase

Jesus was talking to his disciples one day and Peter asked him the following question: "We have left everything to follow you. What then will there be for us?" Jesus said to them, "I tell you the truth, at the renewal of all things, when the Son of Man sits on his glorious throne, you who have followed me will also sit on twelve thrones, judging the twelve tribes of Israel. And everyone who has left houses or brothers or sisters or father or mother or children or fields for my sake will receive **a hundred times as much** and will inherit eternal life. But many who are first will be last, and many who are last will be first" Matthew 19:27-30.

Did you catch that? Peter, speaking for the other 11 disciples is saying that they had left everything to follow Jesus, and basically asks Jesus: "What is in it for us?" That is a blunt, but very fair question that is followed by a very revealing answer. Jesus answers that the disciples who have followed him will sit on twelve thrones alongside him in Heaven and judge the twelve tribes of Israel. Being prophetic, (speaking well into the future at this point), Jesus said that: "**Everyone** who has left houses or brothers or sisters or father or mother or children or fields for my sake will receive a **hundred times as much** and will inherit eternal life." Jesus' disciples (except Judas,) had done that. They left their businesses, their houses, and even some of their family members behind in order to follow Jesus. They were putting Christ first, above everything else in their lives. It means that they followed him even when others tried to convince them that they were making a mistake.

You ask: "Honestly now, what does that really mean for me in the 21st century?" It means that when you exercise XTreme Will, Faith, Obedience, Sacrifice, and Relationship by following Christ in any area of your life, God takes notice and will bless you 100 times as much as it costs you. That certainly would include presenting 10% of your income as a tithe to God as well. Does that mean that God will match my gift 100:1? Actually, I think it means that he will bless you with an even higher ratio than that. He may choose to bless you with riches, with great health, with a wonderful family, with a fantastic spouse, with a tremendous job, with happiness, with fame, or with ten thousand other things. That is up to him. Most importantly, you will spend eternity with Jesus in Heaven. I do know one thing for sure: You can't outgive God.

As it is with many things within the Spiritual realm, XTreme Will, Faith, Obedience, Sacrifice, and Relationship will be rewarded with God's XTreme BLESSINGS. Please read Malachi 3 for yourself.

Do you really want to show your money who's boss? This is the single greatest step you could ever take!

PUT GOD TO THE TEST...HE DARES YOU!

Chapter 18
Take Charge of Your Future

Polly was stuck on go and getting nowhere fast. She had married her college sweetheart a year earlier and due to their lavish spending practices, their finances were totally out of control. In fact, they felt that their money, debts, and monthly bills were controlling their lives. Her career had started off well and at first she climbed up the food chain. For the past two years she seems to be locked or frozen in place. She felt like she was in a rut and doesn't have a clue as to how to get out. She heard someone say that "A rut is a grave with both ends kicked out." She wholeheartedly agreed. She definitely feels like she is in a dead end situation. Both Polly and Ted would love to be able to Show Their Money that they are Boss, but they just don't know how to go about doing that and being in charge.

We will come back to Polly and Ted in a minute, but how about you and your life right now? How about your financial situation? Are you exactly where you want to be at this point in your life? If your answer is "Yes," then congratulations are in order. Your hard work, self discipline, motivation, accomplishments, achievements, money management skills, and other personal skills and traits have paid off. If your answer is: "No," like the majority of us, then you still have work remaining to be done. You may feel like you are in the same rut with Polly. Join me in looking at Polly's story as she takes positive steps to get out of her rut. Better still, if you feel that you are in a rut and want to get out, let Polly's story show you how you can get out of your rut.

START BY DREAMING

Dream about where you want your life to be one year from now. Dream about where you would like to be five years from now. While you are dreaming about your future, go ahead and dream about where you want to be in 10 years as well. After you dream about your future, take the next two steps. First, after you have decided what and where you want your life to be five years from today, write your dreams down in a short but detailed list. Second, map out a strategy to help get you there.

Every person maps out numerous strategies each and every day. We don't usually call them strategies. We usually call them plans. "Many are the plans in a man's heart, but it is the Lord's purpose that prevails" Proverbs 19:21. You and I don't necessarily call it planning, but we plan many activities every day. We plan the time for the alarm to wake us; we plan what to wear; we plan what time to leave for work, which route to take, and what stops to make along the way; we prioritize our daily work schedules; we plan what to eat for lunch; we plan to stop at the grocery store on the way home, and what we will prepare for dinner; we plan what to watch on TV; and we plan what time we will go to bed.

We plan all the time. We just don't call it planning. The trouble is we sometimes don't like to plan out the big things, the most important things in life. Some of the important things we avoid include things like career choices, changing jobs, seeking a promotion, deciding whom to marry, buying a house, buying a car, and many others. Polly discovered that there were three major reasons people avoid planning life's big issues. She found that she was like many others who seek to avoid planning altogether for fear of these three pitfalls.

1. Some have a deep fear that they will make a big mistake.
2. Some don't know how to plan the big events of life.
3. Some just don't like to plan.

Not having an aim or a plan for her future may be why Polly is stuck in her rut. **NOT HAVING A PLAN IS LIKE:**
- Building a house without a blueprint
- Playing a game of Monopoly without rules
- Sailing a ship without a rudder
- Teaching a child to read without a book
- Driving a car without a steering wheel
- Baking a cake without a recipe

Ted decided to bake a cake and surprise Polly for their first anniversary. Though he had never baked before and didn't have a recipe, he vaguely remembered what he had seen his grandmother do several years earlier. Ted began by sifting five cups of flour into a large mixing bowl. Next he added six eggs and a pound of coconut. He followed that up with two cans of peaches, a banana and peanut butter mashed together, 2 cups of buttermilk, 2 cups of strong coffee, 2 cups of grated carrots, 2 cups of sugar, 1cup of peanuts, 1cup of shredded sweet potato, 1 cup of peanut oil, 1 cup of pumpkin, ½ cup of chopped onion, ½ cup of baking soda, ¼ cup of salt, one stalk of finely chopped celery, half an avocado, one clove of garlic, and a dash of instant potatoes.

Ted was proud of himself as he poured his concoction into three large cake pans, popped them into the oven, and baked them for two hours. He sang his favorite Elvis tunes as he washed the dishes he had dirtied. He was amazed that the kitchen smelled absolutely wonderful as he watched the cakes swell in the oven. The smell reminded him of Thanksgiving; baked sweet potatoes, turkey and dressing, and pumpkin pie. Once, he had to stop and clean the overflow out of the oven. But, when the cakes were finally done, he pulled them out of the oven and let them cool.

For the frosting he used three containers of frozen dairy whip, some maple syrup, and a dash of soy sauce. He soon realized that the frosting was a bit too thin so he added several packets of instant oatmeal to thicken it a bit. The finished product was a beauty. Polly was in for the surprise of her life. Ted didn't know it but so was he.

Please don't try this at home. Silly story? Yes, but it does illustrate what can happen when a person does not have a plan to follow. They add a dash of this and a dash of that, some of something else, and a lot of nothing. Ted's problem was that he had mixed various parts of three or four different recipes together. What resulted was an inedible monstrosity. What do you end up with when you neglect proper planning? Like Ted's cake, it's anybody's guess.

Planning can Accelerate you Toward your Goals

If you aim at nothing, you will hit it every time. All of us have made some major life-altering decisions in the past without planning and understanding the consequences of our decisions. Decisions like buying a car we can't afford; changing jobs without considering the long-term picture; deciding upon a college major with no regard for future employment possibilities; deciding whom to marry based upon all the wrong reasons, and the list goes on and on. Imagine what would happen in your life if you had your eyes opened to the benefits of planning. You would be motivated to begin planning your way toward successfully managing your finances, your career, your spending, your debts, and many other vital areas of your life. In her research, Polly discovered that planning has several components.

A Well Defined Plan Will:
- Clearly define what you are attempting to accomplish
- Be very specific
- Be very realistic
- Be attainable
- Be easily measurable

Every weekend Ted would go to the ATM and withdraw $100 to spend for his lunch, snacks, and gasoline for his work week. Because of the successes Polly was beginning to have due to planning, Ted decided that he wanted to begin cutting back on expenses so he wrote down the following two plans. Note the differences.

Plan A. "I want to spend less money and save more money."

Plan B. "I will start saving $50 per week by taking my lunch to work every day. I will start bringing my snacks from home instead of buying them from the vending machines at work."

Note that both plans are valid and can be made to work with a little effort.

Plan A is not very specific but can be made to work. Non-specific plans like that have worked for many people, perhaps they have even worked for you.

Plan B will work better than plan A because it is a well-defined plan.

Let's analyze plan B. It contains the following five elements:

1. It clearly defines what Ted is attempting to accomplish…*save $50 per week.*

2. It is very specific…*take his lunch and snacks to work, stop buying vending snacks.*

3. It is very realistic…*saving $10 per day is less than he is now spending for food.*

4. It is attainable…*can be easily accomplished; anybody could do this.*
5. It is something easily measured…*Ted can check his billfold on Friday.*

15 Things Planning Can Do For you:
- Accurately states what you expect to accomplish
- Identifies your life's priorities
- Establishes the direction you choose to take with anything you plan
- Keeps you on that path you have chosen
- Eliminates frivolous or petty concerns
- Gives you a definite sense of purpose
- Instills confidence, in God, in yourself, and in your own abilities
- Causes you to examine various options
- Serves as a blueprint for all areas of your life you choose to include
- Helps you know where to invest your resources, time, efforts, and energy
- Keeps you looking forward toward the future, not backward toward the past
- Helps you avoid mistakes and pitfalls
- Identifies your spending priorities
- Keeps your eye on the prize…your goal
- Helps you focus on Jesus, not upon your problems

Planning Doesn't Have to be Complicated

Both Polly and Ted were beginning to see the benefits that planning can bring into their lives. Ted was saving money on food costs, and Polly was beginning to make some plans to get out of her rut at work. To offer her support, she had even managed to eat a small chunk of Ted's Banana Pumpkin Turkey and Dressing Peanut Butter Sweet Potato Carrot "cake."

If you have always been one to fly by the seat of your paints and planning has not been a major priority for you, take heart. While planning may be your least favorite activity, that is fine. Nobody said you had to like it. Start out small and work you way up to larger more detailed plans. Begin by taking small steps. Some of the most successful people in the world have discovered the benefits of completing a daily worksheet or a "To Do" list at the beginning of the day. You may wish to do the same as you begin the planning process. In Chapter 11 we discussed the principles of paying off credit card debt. You may remember the suggestion of starting with your smallest credit card balance and paying it off. After the first card is paid off, you move up to your next largest balance and pay it off. Then you move up to the next card, and so forth. That whole process was a plan. It was a plan to enable a person to get out of debt. It would be impossible to get out of debt without following a plan of some sort.

Translate that planning process into other areas of your life. It is best to start out by taking some small steps that can enable you to reach some early successes with relative ease. Begin by planning some daily and weekly activities and watch them work for a while. By starting with daily and weekly plans before attempting monthly and longer plans, you will build some easy wins into your planning process. Put some successes under your belt. Experiment with and then develop your own style of planning. The goal is for planning to work for you. It doesn't really matter how you do it or what it looks like so long as it works for you.

Go as far as you wish with this. Use as many or as few as you want. Daily Plans, Weekly Plans, Monthly Plans, Three Month Plans, Six Month Plans, One Year Plans, Five Year Plans, and so forth. It is your future, and the more time and effort you can put into it, the better equipped you will be to meet whatever comes your way.

Ted's and Polly's Beach Vacation Plan
- What we want to Accomplish: *Save $1,000 for a beach Vacation.*
- The Plan: *We will save $20.00 per week for one year.*
- The Result: *In one year we will have saved $1,040 for our beach vacation.*
- Why it is Realistic: *We can easily cut back on our weekly spending.*
- What we will do to make it Attainable: *Eat out two less times a week.*

- How we can Measure our success: <u>Monitor our $20.00 savings each week.</u>

Ted and Polly decided to save for a weekend vacation at their favorite beach. They thought it through and wrote it on their planning worksheet. Take a look at the sample planning worksheet. If you have never been a planner, this could be a good starting point for you. If this worksheet is not right for you then change it or design one of your own. The goal is for you to have some sort of planning process that works for you. It does not matter what other people use. You should use any method that works best for you.

NEITHER TWO PEOPLE NOR ANY TWO PLANS ARE ALIKE

The beautiful thing about planning is that your plan doesn't have to be like somebody else's plan. It can and must be uniquely yours. Develop your own personal style by designing your own planning worksheet. Keep it simple: you don't have to rewrite Lincoln's Gettysburg Address. As you begin to plan and gain some success you can further refine your own planning style. The goal at this point is to do something that works for you. Forget about someone else's plans. Concentrate on developing your own plans…those that will work for you and your family.

As you decide upon the plans you want and need to make, be true to yourself and to your Lord. Ask for his guidance. Search the Bible for answers. There are thousands of gems of wisdom and truth awaiting you in the books of Psalms, Proverbs, Matthew, Mark, Luke, and John. After you read and study them, branch out to others. Search these books and find God's gifts awaiting you on each and every page. Discovering God's gifts is like finding sparkling diamonds lying on top of the pages of his Word. "But, I just don't have enough time to do that," some will say. The answer is simple…make more time. "That's impossible, no one can make more time. Don't you know that there are only 24 hours in the day?" By making more time I am saying that you can prioritize your time. You can get up a half hour to one hour earlier, watch one hour less television, play one hour less Xbox, or spend one hour less on your cell phone and use that time with God and his Word. God guarantees that you will benefit yourself 100 times more by spending time with him than you possibly could by doing anything else. **WARNING: YOUR PLANS CAN'T GUARANTEE SUCCESS:**

Ted and Polly were beginning to have successes in their planning so they came up with a super-duper plan they just knew would make them rich and change their lives. However, they needed to learn one major principle about planning: Just because you plan something doesn't guarantee that it will succeed or actually happen. For example, read Ted's and Polly's plan. Is there any guarantee that it will come to fruition if they prayed about it, felt great about it, researched it, wrote it out, and then implemented it?

"We will start our own business, work 80 hours per week every week for the next 10 years, contact 100 prospects per week every single week, grow our business, open 3 additional offices, hire 100 new staff, and retire with ten million dollars ten years from today."

Ted and Polly had a bang-up plan. It even met the simple criteria of their planning worksheet. Is it a sound plan?

- Clearly defines what they are attempting to accomplish… *start our own business*
- Is very specific…*retire in 10 years with 10 million dollars*
- Is very realistic…*contact 100 prospects per week*
- Is attainable…*with lots of hard work this is possible for us to accomplish*
- Is something easily measured…*we will know the results in ten years*

Ted and Polly had an ambitious plan. It was a good plan that had the potential of offering many successes. However, there is absolutely **no guarantee** that their plan will succeed. There are scores of things that could affect their plan and keep it from being realized. The first one being that this plan is far too shallow for such an ambitious goal. For a plan like this to have a realistic shot at success, the business owner would need a well-designed and highly detailed business plan. A business plan of this magnitude could only be developed after having done many hours of research, knowing everything about their product, knowing the competition they were facing, and knowing the market they were attempting to serve. Their plan would have to outline almost every conceivable step which would need to be taken to start their business; to grow their business; and to sustain the viability of their business. In addition, they would have to have the right products or services; they would have to be located in a buyer's market for their products or services; they would have to actually work very hard not just say that they would work hard; they would have to outpace their competition; they would have to follow their well-executed business plan; and they would have to be good businesspeople with good business sense. Similar plans like theirs are devised and followed each day. Some succeed and some do not. There are many factors that can either make or break a plan. Success is not guaranteed; it is planned for and earned by a lot of hard work.

DON'T BE DISCOURAGED

Just because Ted's and Polly's plan is very ambitious and larger than life doesn't mean that it can't happen. There are a myriad of success stories about men and women just like them who do great things in business. Success can and does happen. I hope that it happens for you. Realistically, a great plan does not guarantee success. Some great plans are worth no more than the paper they are written upon.

A great plan is nothing more than a great plan. A great plan that SUCCEEDS, does so because someone had a dream, translated their dream into a well-developed plan, implemented their plan with great execution, the right people, lots of hard work, the right product or service, and the right marketing.

Don't be afraid to plan big plans. You may have one of the greatest ideas on the planet. Your idea may be something that will work. Have you ever heard of Microsoft's Bill Gates, Apple Computer's Steve Jobs, or EBay's Meg Whitman? They had a few things in common. Each one of them began with a great idea. Each one of them took their great idea and further developed it. Finally, after further developing and refining their ideas, they implemented them, worked hard, and watched them succeed. You may just be the next success story and be the one to follow the same process followed by these highly successful people. Don't be afraid to plan big, but be realistic, be balanced, and start out with the small things first. I am sure that none of the three highly successful people mentioned above ever envisioned where their plan would take them when they first started. **"Expect Great things From God; Attempt Great things For God."**

Ted and Polly learned a lot about planning. She did a lot of soul-searching and climbed up out of her rut she was in. Ted learned that he could save $50 a week by taking his lunch to work. Polly was so inspired that she began taking her lunch with her as well. They saved their money and were able to take a vacation. However, it was not a weekend trip to their favorite beach. They had saved enough that they decided to fly to the Caribbean and do some snorkeling, fishing, and sunning for a week. While at the beach they decided that they had finally learned how to show their money that they were boss. They also realized that they probably couldn't make $10 million dollars in ten years with the plan they wrote. But they are working on a business plan today and are planning to start their own business in early 2010. Life goes on…they are truly happy with the way things have worked out since they started involving God and each other in all their plans.

Chapter 19
Becoming the Successful Person You were Meant to Be

With the exception of Jesus, every person who ever lived has experienced failures in their lives. I have experienced many failures; my wife points them out all the time. No…I'm just joking! I am joking about the fact that she points them out all the time. I am blessed with a wonderful wife who NEVER points them out. The point is that both you and I have failed more times than we care to count. So What? We are human. The Lord had something to say about all of this in Psalm 103. Read if for yourself. Just because we experience failures does not mean that we are a failure. Far from it. Every successful person you can point to has failed many times in their lives. That doesn't make them a failure…it makes them a human just like you and me.

Hallmarks of Success

Everyone encounters financial storms. During a hurricane, a tornado, or a blizzard any sensible person knows to run for cover. Like an experienced sailor who is accidentally caught at sea by a sudden storm, many have learned that the best response for surviving financial storms is not to run from them, but to meet them squarely head-on. They acknowledge them, analyze them, embrace them, and then defeat them. Many people that have discovered these secrets of successful money management know how to show their money who's boss. They are usually exceptional money managers, and they weigh in at all socio-economic levels.

By applying the principles of *Showing Your Money Who's Boss*, you can become a successful money manager. Certain hallmarks of success separate exceptional money managers from the pack. These hallmarks are the tactics that savvy managers employ in response to life's storms. Wise managers make deliberate and informed choices. The pack relies upon accidental or lucky decisions. Successful managers transcend a survival state of mind and develop winning solutions. The pack is content to allow someone to do their thinking for them. Experienced managers draw from deep sources of inner strength. The pack relies upon emotionally based surface-level feelings. Creative managers command the use of every available resource at their disposal. The pack settles for those that are readily available. Informed managers accurately assess their situation and devise plans that will enable them to excel. The pack sits back and waits to see what will happen. Goal-oriented managers focus all their strengths and energies on achieving lasting results. The pack wallows in worthless self-pity. Insightful managers conserve every available resource until it is needed most. The pack wastes or squanders their limited resources. Teachable managers know how to apply survival techniques that can be learned by anyone, including you and your family. The pack sits back and waits to be rescued.

Life is all about survival, but life is also so much more than just survival. Life is far too short for us to be satisfied to merely eke out an existence and just get by. At times, too many of us have experienced that level of living. **Show Your Money Who's Boss** is a call to action. It was written to equip you to go beyond simply surviving your financial storms, for exceptional managers are never content to reside at that level. They go far beyond simple survival and climb to a much more rewarding and higher level of living…living life to its fullest. Show Your Money Who's Boss!

Addendum

For additional valuable resources visit a few of my favorite Christian websites…

www.biblegateway.com
www.christianretirement.com
www.christiansunited.com
www.focusonthefamily.com
www.gracetoyou.com
www.intouch.org
www.oneplace.com
www.rbc.org
www.samaritanspurse.org

www.ingramcontent.com/pod-product-compliance
Lightning Source LLC
Chambersburg PA
CBHW071418170526
45165CB00001B/319